DOG TALES

SUSY FLORY

HARVEST HOUSE PUBLISHERS

EUGENE, OREGON

Published in association with MacGregor Literary, Portland, Oregon

Cover photo © iStockphoto / PK-Photos

Backcover author photo © Flory Photo

Cover design by Left Coast Design, Portland, Oregon

DOG TALES
Copyright © 2011 by Susy Flory
Published by Harvest House Publishers
Eugene, Oregon 97402
www.harvesthousepublishers.com

Library of Congress Cataloging-in-Publication Data
Flory, Susy.
Dog tales / Susy Flory.
    p. cm.
ISBN 978-0-7369-2987-5 (pbk.)
1. Dogs—Anecdotes. 2. Human–animal relationships—Anecdotes. I. Title.
SF426.2.F56 2011
636.7—dc22

2010047852

For Doug Foxworthy, a dear friend, brother, and fellow dog lover, and his amazing wife, Sherry. I'll never forget our team's adventures in Cuba, including Doug's Spanglish, his crazy morning jogs in Havana while smoking a cigar and dodging Cuban troops, and the incredible miracle of Sandy's torn pants.

Also, for Joe, Nannette, and Hunter.
Of all the stories in this book, yours most touched my heart.

Acknowledgments

Thanks to my family—Robert, Ethan, Teddy, and Mom—for being ever patient as I told dog story after dog story around the kitchen table. Thanks for loving me, encouraging me, and celebrating with me. Boudin, anyone?

Angela, thanks for baking me a blackberry and apple pie at deadline time. You are a love.

Thanks to Chip MacGregor, agent extraordinaire, for sparking the idea for this book and for being a truth-teller and my voice of wisdom.

And to LaRae Weikert. Thanks for falling in love with this little dog book. It's an honor to work with you and the rest of the team at Harvest House.

To Barb Gordon, my editor and fellow cowgirl. I'm grateful for your astute guidance and sharp pencil.

Hugs to my 9-1-1 crew, Tracy, Claire, Janet A, Shirley, Shannon, Bea, Janet C, and the whole Flory and Kuzmicky family. I could not have survived this past year without you.

Love to my prayer partners Diane, Anita, Gini, Barbara Sue, Kathi, Margaret, and Sara. I know you always have my back.

Thank you Mark, my pastor and friend. I appreciate your guidance and your prayers.

My dear friends at Neighborhood Church, thank you for being there in tangible ways for us this past year. Tammy, Annette, Rita, and Diane, I cherish your friendship and love you all.

And Jeannie, thanks for the gift of Sprinkles. She came at just the right time. She adds sunshine to our lives.

Contents

Terrier Therapy

~~≈~~

Don't worry...I'm here. The floodwaters will recede,
the famine will end, the sun will shine tomorrow,
and I will always be here to take care of you.

<small>CHARLIE BROWN TO SNOOPY</small>

I had a blister on the back of my ankle recently. It was painful, the kind of blister that is raw and red. I earned it when I was in Dallas on a business trip, staying at a big hotel set up for large conventions. It was a beautiful place, with large echo-y atriums full of ivy, giant Buddhas, and elephant statues. Out back was a sculpture garden with bronze statues of children flying kites and catching butterflies. Around the sculpture garden was a jogging track with a synthetic springy surface that looked like a fresh slice of warm carrot cake with cream cheese frosting. (Just from that simile you can probably understand why I needed to be out on that track, walking my double chin off.) Overlooking the garden, in a building separate from the hotel, was a gym.

One morning I was feeling particularly ambitious and I got up early, drank some juice, ate a banana, and pulled on my workout clothes. Just a few weeks before, I had run (I use the term "run" loosely) in my very first race, a 5K (approximately three miles) to benefit the sports program for

7

my daughter's high school. To prepare for the race, I had purchased an expensive pair of running socks with pads on the toes and ankles. The socks were a cool shade of silvery blue and green. I pranced through the atriums and deserted lobbies on my way to the gym. I was just a little bit proud of myself. *Look at me. I'm going to work out in my new padded running socks!*

I headed out the back doors, and the hot and heavy air engulfed me. *Whew. I'm glad the gym is air-conditioned.* Inside the building that housed the gym, I stretched my legs while I talked to the attendant. She directed me to sign in and then asked if I wanted the charge put on my hotel bill. *Charge?* I was dismayed when she explained that guests at the hotel had to pay for a workout. Irritated, I said, "No thanks," turned on my padded running socks, and headed to the sculpture garden. *Humph! I'll just work out for free on the carrot cake track.*

I walked for a while to warm up and then began a slow jog. Every once in a while I stopped to adjust my iPod (meaning: to catch my breath) or take a drink of water (meaning: to try to stop breathing so hard). I sped up in the shade and slowed down in the sun and had a lovely time. For free. The only problem was that the heat caused my feet to swell a bit and my expensive socks slipped down, which meant my shoe rubbed the back of my ankle. It stung but I ignored it and kept going. After a few more laps, I headed inside. I started limping when I hit the Buddhas. When I passed the elephant statue I repented of my slight air of superiority about working out. And by the time I made it back to my room, it was clear I had a pretty nasty blister. You know what they say—everything's bigger in Texas.

After a quick application of Neosporin and a Band-Aid, I went on with my day. Blisters heal slowly, and it still looked pretty nasty by the time I got home. I kept it covered with bandages and tried to forget about it.

The morning after I got home, I was standing in front of the mirror in my pink fuzzy robe and brushing my wet hair. I felt something strange on the back of my ankle. It didn't hurt exactly. It felt warm and tickly. I looked down and Sprinkles, our six-month-old silky terrier puppy, was licking my wound.

I wasn't sure whether to yell at her because it was kind of gross or just say, "Aw, thank you, honey." Sprinkles was doing what dogs are born to do—take care of us. No one has really nailed down the definitive history of dogs. No one is quite sure who first domesticated the gray wolf, the ancestor of the dog, but for the last 15,000 years dogs have been used across the world for hunting, herding, protection, military purposes, and companionship. No other domesticated animal has earned the term "man's best friend." Dogs and people just go together.

And the blister incident wasn't just a one-time thing with Sprinkles. Every morning she waited for the moment when I would leave the shower to brush my hair and put on makeup. As soon as I got distracted, she wanted to help my blister heal. She was persistent. She was diligent. That little puppy was going to fix my blister, darn it!

The blister finally healed, and Sprinkles stopped her fixation with the back of my ankle. And to be honest, I sort of missed it. I felt loved, like she had been trying her best to connect with me, to take care of me, to heal me. I think that canine drive to bond and to nurture gets at the core of why we love dogs. There is a special kind of connection and interdependence between a human and a dog when the relationship is working right. And in that interdependence, there is health, and hope, and healing.

Sprinkles came into our family at a critical moment and she has turned out to be our unofficial therapy dog. There's something about stroking her back that is soothing. She greets everyone at the front door with a tail wag and a smile. She makes me laugh when her terrier genes emerge and she shakes her toy to kill it or when she busily digs a hole in the side yard, front paws going 90 miles an hour. When we go on walks, her joy is infectious. She is a bright spot always. After a difficult year for our family, she has helped us—all of us—heal.

When I'm working, Sprinkles sleeps on a Snoopy pillow under my desk or plays with a squeaky stuffed toy. I recorded a bunch of phone interviews for the dog stories in this book, and when I listened back I could often hear her little terrier growl while she shook a squeaky toy. While writing, I often reached my foot out to nudge her, reminding myself she was there.

Even as I worked on the last chapter and began to cry a bit as I wrote about my dad, she came out of nowhere and jumped up on my lap. Often when my heart was especially touched by a tender story, I would pet her for a while. Sprinkles would give me a doggie kiss or two with her cute little tongue. Then she'd get down and go about her day. Her presence touches something deep inside me, where the emotional and spiritual wounds hide deep.

The dogs in this book are like Sprinkles. On the surface they are bundles of fur and wagging tails and stinky dog breath. But they are so much more. They are survivors, healers, therapists, friends, protectors, playmates, caretakers, and rescuers. Sometimes they are gentle, and sometimes they are fierce. Sometimes they make us laugh; sometimes they make us cry. Sometimes we teach them, and sometimes they teach us. They forgive and forget, they love without expectation, and they always live in the moment.

All the stories in this book are true, down to the last detail. Some of the stories have strong elements of faith, some highlight the working relationships between humans and dogs, and some of them are just dogs being dogs. My working title for this book was "Dog Miracles," and that's exactly how I think of the extraordinary dogs you are about to encounter. I've fallen in love with each and every one, and I hope you will too.

Buddy's Big Adventure

*One does not discover new lands
without consenting to lose sight
of the shore for a very long time.*

André Gide

Beagles are prone to wanderlust. Buddy knows a thing or two about the adventure. He is a four-year-old beagle who lives on a one-acre property with four other dogs in Eatontown, New Jersey, a quiet town about an hour's drive south of New York City. Buddy lives with his family, including Charlie Kelley, who retired from the computer business and now sells real estate.

Buddy's not much of a dog-toy lover. Instead, his hobby is patrolling the fence. "We live on a corner," said Charlie. "We have a fence lining the property, and he likes to run along that and bark and howl when people walk by. It's his favorite thing in the world to do, just running up and down along the fence following them."

Besides wanderlust, beagles are also known for stubborn independence and a thirst for adventure. They love to eat and will do almost anything for food. "Buddy's favorite food is F-O-O-D," Charlie added.

Beagles were originally bred to be hunters, running cross-country chasing after rabbits and foxes. Combine all of that beagle energy with a visit to a busy dog beach on a summer afternoon, and you have a strong likelihood that something unplanned and unexpected will take place—beagle style. And that's just what happened to Buddy one afternoon in August.

There's a dog beach called Fisherman's Cove down on the Jersey Shore, by a place called Manasquan. The dog beach goes down to the bay inlet where water comes in from the harbor and goes out to the ocean. It's a busy place, and dogs are supposed to be leashed. Most people let their dogs run free to frolic on the beach and play in the water.

Charlie's son Patrick and two granddaughters, Alyssa and Shannon, took Buddy to the beach and put him on a long rope so he could explore. At first he had a great time running in and out of the water. But then he started getting nervous. "He's sociable with people and animals he knows," explained Charlie. "But when something new comes on the scene and too much is happening around him, he is standoffish and wants to check out."

That day the activity had climbed to a level that made Buddy uncomfortable so the Kelleys decided to head home. They reeled Buddy in on the long rope and held him close. Patrick untied the rope and was about to snap on his regular leash when it happened. Another dog had gotten loose and the owner, in hot pursuit, bumped into Buddy. That did it.

"He freaked out and took off down the beach," Charlie said.

The Kelleys ran after him, frantically calling, but they quickly lost sight of the fleeing beagle. They had no idea where he'd gone. They only knew the general direction he'd started in. They drove around the area just outside the beach, looking and calling—but there was no beagle response. And no one had seen him. Patrick and the girls called Charlie and his wife, Edie, to tell them what had happened. The two grandparents jumped in the car and drove over to help. After a long search, they all left for home with heavy hearts. Their only consolation was that Buddy was so cute someone was bound to find him and take him in.

Although they lived 25 minutes away from Manasquan, the Kelleys went back to the area every single day for the next three weeks. They scoured the beach and surrounding area. They put posters up everywhere, talked to the police to see if there were any beagle sightings, and posted "lost dog" announcements all over the Internet.

At first they received a large number of leads. Every beagle owner they met said, "I'm not surprised he ran away." Beagles are independent and stubborn with loads of energy. They're also known as explorers and chasers who follow their noses. Apparently beagles with wanderlust are legion.

"We got dozens of calls saying 'I saw this beagle here' and 'I saw this beagle there,'" Charlie said. "We checked out every lead, and it never turned out to be Buddy."

Their persistence led them to search a ten-mile radius around the beach. They also called police departments and road departments to see if there were any reports of a beagle being hit by a car. The Kelleys didn't give up the hunt, but they did finally stop going to the beach every day. Their visits dwindled to two or three times a week, but they never stopped hoping. "We didn't get bad news so we kept going," Charlie shared. When the leads thinned out, they offered a $500 reward. A local attorney and pet lover anonymously matched the $500 to make it $1000.

One day after Buddy had been gone for about two months, the Kelleys got a good tip. Charlie received a call from a fisherman coming in from the ocean. He had been motoring down the channel into the harbor near the dog beach and saw a dog on Gull Island, a 48-acre land mass near the Manasquan Inlet. It's deserted except for large flocks of seagulls that congregate on the sandbars at low tide to gobble down clams and crabs.

The Kelleys raced to their car and drove down to the Jersey Shore to check out the lead. "We didn't see any possibility that Buddy could be on that island, but we were going to check it out," Charlie said. "There was no access except by boat as far as we could tell." And there was no way he could have made it to the island by swimming. The current in the inlet was too strong even for a dog that was a good swimmer, and Buddy was the type of dog who only liked to get his feet wet.

When they arrived at the beach they didn't see any sign of Buddy. Although it was unlikely that Buddy swam to the island, it wasn't impossible. Most dogs can swim instinctively. A couple of years ago an extraordinary story came out of England. A lifeboat crew was two and a half miles out at sea on a rescue mission when they saw a dog out in the water by itself, struggling to stay afloat.[1] The crew hauled the dog, a female Staffordshire bull terrier named Kelly, aboard the boat. Like Buddy, Kelly had been walking on the beach when she chased some seagulls and ran away. She disappeared and her owners spent hours looking for her. The lifeboat crew took her to the local Society for the Prevention of Cruelty to Animals (SPCA), and since Kelly was wearing ID, they notified the police. The police called Kelly's family, who quickly picked up their dog. If an elderly bull terrier could swim miles out to sea, it wasn't inconceivable that Buddy could do something similar.

A week later, there was another dog sighting. A second fisherman who had seen the "lost dog" posters saw a dog on Gull Island. "I *know* it's a beagle," he told Charlie. He offered to take the family over on his boat. They went along and searched the beach side of the island, calling and calling. No Buddy. But an important piece of information emerged. The fisherman mentioned that at certain times of day when the tides were low, there was access to Gull Island by following a set of railroad tracks, crossing a swampy area, and then climbing up the big hill on the backside.

The sightings reenergized the search, and the New Jersey State Police, Marine Patrol Division, sent a search team to the island. In addition, the Coast Guard station at Point Pleasant had reported dog sightings on security cameras pointed at the island. There was definitely a beagle over there. They even observed him dragging around some dead seagulls.

Almost three months had passed since the day Buddy ran away. The multiple beagle sightings "really perked our ears." The Kelleys began to visit the island regularly. One day, they spotted Buddy through binoculars. He was out on a sandbar but wouldn't come even though they yelled themselves hoarse. They decided to explore the island more thoroughly. The day after Thanksgiving, along with friends and family, they walked the railroad tracks and found a clearing through the marsh. Once on the island, they looked and called Buddy's name again and again without response. They repeated their search for the next two days, checking the tide schedule to make sure they could get across the swampy area between the railroad tracks and the steep hill.

Now that they knew Buddy was alive and on Gull Island, the Kelleys worried about the upcoming bad weather. "We were getting into December, and the forecast was calling for cold and snow," said Charlie. With the beagle likely in a weakened condition from exposure, along with the lack of food and fresh water, Buddy would probably not survive an Atlantic winter.

Then an unlikely hero named "Muskrat Jack" stepped in. Jack Neary serves as the local animal control officer in Manasquan. "He is a colorful character," said Charlie. "He's 62 years old, a rugged guy, and a fisherman. He told me he started trapping animals with his dad when he was nine years old." Muskrat Jack offered to set a live animal trap on Gull Island to try to catch Buddy. The Kelleys were ecstatic.

Muskrat Jack visited Gull Island for some reconnaissance and spotted Buddy. The beagle ran by him "like a Greyhound," he told a reporter for the Star News Group.

"There is no way to catch him once he takes off running," Charlie confirmed, "especially if he senses people are chasing him."

But Buddy had a weakness. It was the beagle's Achilles heel, his Samson-like weakness, his Kryptonite: F-O-O-D. Drawing from his long years of experience, Muskrat Jack unleashed his secret weapon: a special bait that is, well, secret. At three o'clock in the afternoon on December 7, three months after Buddy ran away, Muskrat Jack set the trap on Gull Island. It didn't take long. A little later that afternoon,

Buddy went for the bait. Edie Kelley, Charlie's wife, got the good news by phone. "Muskrat Jack caught him!" she yelled.

Buddy had been gone 98 days.

The Kelleys drove down to the beach parking lot to meet Muskrat Jack. "We thought he was sent from heaven," Charlie commented. Buddy was emaciated—down to 19 pounds from his original 35. One of Charlie's daughters works for a veterinary clinic, so she asked the vet if he would come in and check Buddy. Charlie and Edie rushed Buddy in, and the vet looked him over while Charlie and his family waited with thumping hearts. They knew there was very little fresh water on Gull Island, and with hardly anything for him to eat, they were sure the news would be bad. Then the vet came in to announce the results of the exam, and it was completely unexpected. "There was hardly anything wrong with him!" Charlie said. His blood work was a little off, but nothing that wouldn't sort it itself out as Buddy rested and regained his body weight. "He's an amazing dog—just very skinny," Charlie said.

Home again, Buddy settled back into his routine: eating, sleeping, hanging out with his family, playing with the other dogs, and patrolling the fence around the yard. After talking to Muskrat Jack and the other fishermen, the Kelleys solved the mystery of how Buddy found water. The water flowing by Gull Island is salt water mixed with fresh, called "brack" or "brackish" water from the Dutch *brak,* which means "salt." The level of salinity in the water is somewhere between freshwater and saltwater. It's unpleasant to drink and can cause health problems, but Buddy must have hit a spot with drinkable water where the river flows into the ocean. "He got lucky," said Charlie.

And as far as F-O-O-D, there was plenty of it, enough to support hundreds of seagulls. Buddy probably ate clams and sand crabs on the sandbars at low tide just like the birds. There's also a good chance he sampled some ripe seagull meat along the way.

Buddy's big adventure impacted the Kelleys "in such a funny way," said Charlie. "First, just the experience of looking for him every day drew us closer together. Our granddaughters were very close to the dog.

We were together right after the dog ran away, and we stayed together looking for him. But when three weeks became a month, and then six weeks, and then eight, it's hard to stay up and positive. But we did it. It was an example to our two granddaughters not to give up looking and not to give up hope. It was a good lesson for Patrick and us too."

Buddy's capture and safe return validated the family's faith. "It was a gift from heaven at Christmastime," Charlie said. After Buddy came home, the winter weather settled in and temperatures dropped to 20 degrees. Out on Gull Island, Buddy probably would not have survived.

Buddy the Beagle has since regained the weight he lost on his escapade and is back to good health. And when the Kelleys go to the dog beach, they make sure he is safely strapped into a new, sturdy harness.

When Buddy's big adventure and the happy ending hit the media, NBC and other major media outlets came calling. A few days after the end of Buddy's ordeal, Fox News sent a limousine to pick up Buddy and the Kelleys for a Sunday morning news show. "On a desert island one week and the next week in a limo in midtown Manhattan," Charlie observed, laughing. "Unreal."

After the experience was over and life got back to normal, Charlie wrote a book called *Buddy the Beagle: The Lost Journey.* If you're ever in Manasquan, New Jersey, stop in at Booktowne on Main Street and pick up a copy. You can also find it on Amazon.com. The book ends with: "Well, now I'm home with my family and my doggie brother, Sunny. I've been eating real well and gaining back some of my lost weight. I am just enjoying life. And I promise to never run away again."

We're holding you to that, Buddy.

Champp and the .45

~~✦~~

Dogs are miracles with paws.
SUSAN ARIEL RAINBOW KENNEDY

It was a chilly spring evening when Tiffany went out to the kennel to bring Champ inside. Tiffany is the founder of the Coastal German Shepherd Rescue in Irvine, California, and she's always been an animal lover. "As a child, I would bring home stray kittens and birds," said Tiffany. "I still love rescuing animals. It's a passion that's sort of like an addiction. There are so many animals that need help."

Tiffany looked in at Champ. He was a fluffy golden German shepherd mix with a black muzzle and a golden ruff of fur around his neck like a lion. Champ held a very special place in her heart. She was hoping to find a good, safe home for him soon where he could heal and recover from his violent past. He was a quiet, gentle dog who had been through so much. But on this night, Champ surprised her. When she opened the kennel door, he growled at her.

Dogs growl for a variety of reasons, Tiffany had learned. It's a primal noise that vibrates in the air, raising the skin on the back of your neck. Each type of growl comes with its own message and body language.[1]

- The mean growl means the dog is in attack mode and is usually accompanied by raised hackles and a stiff tail. This means the dog is focused on you and is saying, "If you come closer, I will bite you."

- The warning or defensive growl comes from a frightened dog on the defensive. The dog will sometimes lean or squat back away from you. His behavior is hard to predict. He probably doesn't want to fight but may attack as a bluff.

- A play growl is normal communication for dogs who are wrestling or playing with a toy. It's sort of like basketball players talking back and forth during a game.

- The talking growl is used by some dogs to get their owners' attention when they need to go outside or want to play fetch.

Dogs have a large growl vocabulary, so it's important to study their body language and know what the different movements and postures mean.

In this case, Champ's growl sounded like a combination of a warning growl and an offensive growl. Tiffany figured it was a result of the recent trauma he'd been through. She broke down and cried. "I was just really, really worried that we weren't going to be able to rehabilitate him. And in the ten years I've been doing dog rescue, I've never really felt like that about a dog. I wondered if we were going to be able to save this dog."

Champ first came to Tiffany's attention when an email from a South Los Angeles county animal shelter landed in her inbox. The email contained a shocking plea from a shelter worker asking for rescue for a dog who was slated to be euthanized. The dog was in pretty bad shape. Champ had been shot at least five times in a home invasion robbery, according to an initial report from the Los Angeles Police Department.

"We've taken in dogs that had wounds from BB guns and even pellet guns," said Tiffany. "But this was the first dog I'd encountered who had this type of bullet wounds. I get pleas from lots of animal shelters, and to get one that said a dog had been shot five times was pretty startling and unusual."

Not much is known about the night Champ almost died. In late February, the police in Los Angeles had been contacted by Champ's owners, who reported their dog had been shot. South Los Angeles is a large area southwest and southeast of downtown Los Angeles, home to more than 500,000 people. South Los Angeles used to be known as South Central Los Angeles, but in an effort to improve the city's reputation, the name was changed because "South Central" had become closely associated with gang warfare, poverty, and urban decay. Widespread unemployment and poverty helped spawn several infamous and bloodthirsty gangs, including the notorious Bloods and the Crips. Tension between Black and Latino gangs has prompted racially motivated gang violence there since the early 1990s, with drug activity fueling criminal behavior.

The numbers help tell the story. The Los Angeles Police Department reports more than 250 active gangs in the city of Los Angeles, with a combined membership of over 26,000 people. In the last five years, gang members were responsible for 784 homicides, nearly 12,000 felony assaults, 10,000 robberies, and just under 500 rapes.[2]

Somehow Champ was swept up in this epidemic of drug-fueled violence. It's possible the dog was a hero, shot while defending his owners or his house during a robbery. It's not at all unlikely that Champ was standing his ground and protecting his family even after being shot multiple times. German shepherds were originally bred in Northern Europe to protect flocks of sheep, and modern-day uses for the breed include police and security work, along with serving as Seeing Eye dogs. German shepherds have a good sense of right and wrong and can tell if something is not as it should be. They are loyal, fearless, and dedicated—sometimes too dedicated.

Whatever happened that night in South Los Angeles, Champ

ended up being shot five or six times in the face, neck, shoulder, and abdomen. All the bullets passed through his body and exited except for one. Champ had a .45-caliber slug lodged in his jaw, just under his eye. "An inch over and the bullet in his jaw could have gone to his brain," a veterinarian told the *Orange County Register*, a local newspaper.

"It's sort of crazy that it didn't kill him," Tiffany said.

When the police responded to the call about Champ, the owners released the dog to them, probably because of his extensive injuries and an inability to pay for treatment. Los Angeles Police slapped an evidence hold on the dog and delivered Champ to the county shelter where he would remain until the hold was lifted. (In any criminal case that involves an animal, the animal becomes evidence until such time as the police have the proof they need to proceed with the case. It was possible Champ could prove to be an important piece of evidence, so he was in limbo, forced to remain at the county animal shelter until the police decided they didn't need him anymore.)

"The unfortunate thing is that the county animal shelter didn't have the ability to provide much medical treatment other than antibiotics and a little pain medication here and there," Tiffany said. For ten days Champ waited, bullet in his jaw, for the evidence hold to be released. Finally, on March 9, he was released. The police hadn't identified any suspects. They explained to Tiffany that Champ came from an area with heavy gang activity and everyone was afraid to talk.

The good news is that Champ was free. The bad news is that due to his extensive injuries, his new owner, Los Angeles Animal Control, slated the dog for euthanasia. That's when Tiffany received the email.

"I got the email and thought, *How wrong is this? The dog had been subjected to a crime, sat and suffered for 14 days, and now they're just going to kill him.* She researched his case, gathering information from the shelter. Officials there felt Champ was a nice dog who had suffered a great deal but wasn't salvageable because of what he had gone through.

"He was growling at staff, who had a hard time doing anything with him," Tiffany explained. "I can pretty much understand that. Being shot five times and then put in a cage, I'd be pretty unhappy too!"

When Tiffany first went to the shelter to pick up Champ, she immediately felt a bond with him. "This dog comes limping out with all these wounds," she said. "He's got all these things going against him. Yet he's wagging his tail, and he wanted to come up and lean against me."

She looked down at him, amazed. As he leaned against her leg, she thought, *You're a total champ. You've been through a terrible ordeal and look at you!*

The name stuck.

Due to the shoulder wound, Champ was limping, favoring his left front leg. Shelter officials warned Tiffany an amputation might be necessary. When she tried to put a leash over his head, he flinched, growled, and whimpered. The bullet still lodged in his face was causing significant pain.

When Champ was originally shot, he may not have noticed the injuries at first. It's likely his adrenaline was flowing, and he was growling and barking, knowing instinctively that he and his family were in danger. Most people who have been shot don't realize it until they see the entry wound or the blood. They say it feels like they've been punched.

Most of the pain from a gunshot wound comes afterward. Nerves wake up and scream, letting the body know an injury has occurred. As the days passed, Champ's jaw became inflamed as his body rejected the foreign object embedded in bone and flesh. Champ must have been in a great deal of pain. Eating, drinking, and sleeping would have been very difficult, if not impossible.

After Tiffany checked the dog out of the animal shelter, she took Champ straight to one of the vets she works with. They decided the first task was to remove the bullet. The surgery was fairly simple and straightforward. The surgeon was able to follow the path of the bullet, removing bone fragments as he came across them. The problem was the bullet itself. It was embedded in Champ's jaw and because of the delay in treatment, the wound had started to heal and new tissue was growing over and around it. "It took the surgeon 30 minutes of prying at the bullet to get it out of his jawbone," Tiffany said. "That's how embedded it was. He gave me the bullet, and it was all marked up from the surgeon trying to get it out." Tiffany turned the bullet over to the police department as evidence.

The rest of Champ's bullet wounds were treated and cleaned up. X-rays on his shoulder showed nothing wrong with the bones in his shoulder or his leg. No amputation would be necessary. His limping was probably due to nerve damage.

"We decided we were going to wait and see what happened," Tiffany said. Eventually the shoulder wound healed and Champ's limp went away.

While Champ's body healed, Tiffany and then a foster home volunteer worked on the invisible injuries. Champ was very afraid. "He was friendly and you could tell he very much wanted to trust us," Tiffany said. "But if I made any quick movements or moved to touch him around his neck or face, he would definitely growl."

She didn't give up on him. "You could tell it was out of fear—not that he was an aggressive dog or wanted to hurt me. He was just very afraid." They worked on socialization, meeting new people and new animals, and using a lot of positive reinforcement.

Then came that night at the kennel when Champ growled at her. Fox News had invited her up to Los Angeles for an interview. They were sending a car the next day. Tiffany was worried about the media coverage. Champ's story was beginning to stir up public interest. Reporters wanted to meet Champ, and photographers wanted photos. Tiffany was worried that Champ wasn't ready for the attention because "he was still really sensitive about having people around him and near his face."

When Champ growled at her, Tiffany was devastated, questioning everything. She looked in Champ's eyes and could see the trauma he had been through. She wondered what would happen to this dog and if it had been the right decision to rescue him from being put down. *Would Champ always be afraid? After what had happened, would he ever be able to forget the past and trust people again?*

Then she made a decision. "I cancelled the Fox news interview because I didn't think we could go to Los Angeles and be live on camera," said Tiffany. "If something happened, how terrible would that be? I felt awful, but it was the best thing for him."

The next day, she took the time to hang out with the dog all day. Champ acted just fine. He had turned a corner and the ferocious warning growls never happened again. "I think he was just having a bad night," Tiffany said.

But when she thinks back on that night, it became an epiphany for Tiffany. "It really reinforced for me that all of these dogs can be rehabilitated. It's not about a bad dog—it's about bad humans that do this to dogs." Tiffany believes that with time and patience, "up to 99.9 percent of these guys can be saved."

It wasn't long before Champ found a home. A couple from Washington State contacted the rescue group. They drove to California, met Champ, and fell in love with him. Then it was time for a road trip. They took two weeks and drove up the coast with him, making a vacation out of it. Champ thoroughly enjoyed himself, meeting all kinds of new people and seeing new places along the way. The couple who adopted him has some acreage, and Tiffany enjoys receiving pictures of a healthy, happy Champ romping in the grass with his new buddy, a Rottweiler mix. Champ has also befriended the couple's two cats. He's come a long way from that nightmarish night in South Los Angeles. His scars are barely noticeable now.

"You would never know what he's been through," said Tiffany. "He loves people."

There's an extraordinary video on YouTube with footage taken the day Tiffany picked Champ up from the animal shelter. The dog looks unsteady on his feet. He has holes in his body. He still has a bullet in his jaw. But he wags his tail. And he lifts a front paw to shake hands.

Tiffany started rescuing German shepherds ten years ago. She cofounded Coastal German Shepherd Rescue in Irvine, California, about five years ago with two women who share her passion for rescuing dogs. They rescue German shepherds and German shepherd mixes from all over California. "Unfortunately, the shelters here are seriously impacted and animals are euthanized daily," said Tiffany. "We try to save as many as we can." And they do, adopting out 350 dogs a year to safe, healthy, and loving homes.

Although Tiffany lives and breathes animal rescue, she has a day job training elementary school teachers. "Dog rescue is my second full-time job. It's my job I don't get paid for," she says. And her animal job is much needed. While German shepherds make hard-working police and security dogs, as pets they need owners who understand their needs. Bred for high "prey" drives and high activity levels, they can develop behavior problems if they don't have an outlet for their energy. Boredom and loneliness can lead to destructive behavior such as barking, chewing, digging, and aggression. This can lead to chasing bikes and cars and people. German shepherds are people-oriented and have a strong sense of belonging. They can make wonderful pets for responsible owners who take care to train and socialize their dogs. Tiffany works hard to educate the community about German shepherds. And when she helps a dog like Champ find a new life, all the effort is worth it.

3

Don't Mess with the Brute

⚬⚬⚬

Dogs have given us their absolute all...
They serve us in return for scraps.
It is without a doubt the best deal man has ever made.

ROGER CARAS

Brutis was a big mama's boy. "Big" meaning 125 pounds jumping in your lap and no getting him down. And "mama's boy" meaning he followed Fran Oreto around everywhere, including kitchen, car, bed, and even the shower. Of her seven golden retrievers, Brutis was by far her favorite. She called him Brute.

One warm autumn afternoon at her rural Florida home, Fran sat in her yard swing watching her grandchildren play on a swing set under a huge oak tree in the front yard. Angelique was four years old and Lucca, her redheaded younger brother, was two. After a few minutes on the swings, the kids switched to the teeter-totter. Fran relaxed, the warm air lulling her into a state of relaxation. As always, Brute sat next to her on the swing.

Suddenly Brute came alive. In a split second he jumped up and took off like a shot toward the grandkids. Fran knew something was wrong and jumped up too. When she focused on Brute, she saw something that made her chest tighten in panic. "Oh no!" she screamed. "Brute, what's in your mouth?"

She ran toward Brute and saw what he was holding—a coral snake. The 16-inch snake had a black head with red and yellow bands. Eastern coral snakes are notoriously venomous and are part of the *Elapidae* family, which includes the cobra and the deadly black mamba. Fran could see the snake thrashing and coiling, trying to strike Brute. The dog wouldn't let go.

"Release it! Release it!" she yelled as she grabbed Angelique and Lucca and rushed them into the house.

Fran's husband, Mark, came running when he heard Fran's screams. "What is it?" he hollered. Fran told him about the coral snake. Brute stood in the same spot, the snake still in his mouth. He didn't shake it; he had grabbed it and was just holding on.

Golden retrievers are the very definition of loyalty. This breed of dog often serves in search-and-rescue units and as guide dogs, hearing dogs, and therapy dogs. They are amiable, intelligent, and love children, other dogs, cats, and even livestock.

One famous golden retriever named Isabella became known around the world a couple of years ago when she adopted a litter of white tiger cubs at a wildlife park in Caney, Kansas. She nursed the baby tigers along with her own puppies until they were old enough to wean. In 2010 an 18-month-old golden retriever fought off a cougar to save an 11-year-old boy's life in Canada. Goldens seem to have a strong protective instinct, no matter what the risk to themselves.

With the grandchildren safe in the house, Fran went back for her dog. The snake was moving less and appeared to be stunned. Mark asked Fran to get a Ziploc bag. When she returned, he carefully grabbed the snake right behind the head and threw it into the baggie. They put it into the freezer.

Fran took Brute into the house, and within ten minutes he'd collapsed in the living room.

The Oreto family lives on acreage in a semirural part of Florida with plenty of snakes. Along with coral snakes, there are corn snakes, pygmy rattlers, diamondbacks, and king snakes. Fran had always worked hard to keep the dogs away from all snakes because they could not differentiate between the venomous snakes and the harmless ones. She loves her family, she loves her horses, and she loves her dogs. She fiercely cares for them all with equal intensity. But now she was haunted by the thought that Brute had escaped her protective eye. *I did not see that snake. And neither did the kids.* For that she was grateful. Lucca was the type of curious kid who liked to pick up everything and take a good, close look. At two years old, he just might have grabbed the snake if Brute hadn't beaten him to it. The result could have been deadly for such a small child.

Coral snakes are known to be secretive and nonconfrontational. They generally bite only in self-defense. They have small, rear-facing fangs that are permanently erect. This means the snake usually hangs on after biting, injecting as much venom as possible. There are few human fatalities from coral snakes because most people shake them off before they can inject a lethal amount of venom. In addition, the initial bite of a coral snake causes little or no pain, unlike a rattlesnake bite, which causes intense pain and swelling.

But what a coral snakebite lacks in pain, it makes up for in neurotoxicity. If untreated, the neurotoxin disrupts the connections between the brain and the muscles. Symptoms begin with tingling sensations in the extremities, droopy eyelids, double vision. They end with muscular paralysis. Eventually the victim's lungs shut down and respiratory or cardiac failure occurs.

Strangely enough, the results of a coral snakebite can at first be anticlimactic because the symptoms take time to progress—and can be delayed for up to 12 hours. But there was no delay in Brute's case. His immediate collapse was probably due to the snake biting him in the mouth. And because he held on to the snake while Fran rounded up the kids and whisked them into the house, the coral snake probably had time to pump a large amount of venom into Brute's head.

Fran and her husband tried to walk Brute out to her SUV, but they ended up carrying him. They loaded him into the passenger seat and Fran took off down the dirt-and-lime rock road, headed for the emergency vet clinic. On a normal day, Brute usually sat in the passenger seat, head up, seatbelt on, left paw on the center console. If Fran rested her hand on the console while driving, Brute would rest his left paw gently on top of her hand. "It was as if we were on a hot date, and he wanted to hold my hand," she said.

But on this trip Brute was groggy and slumped down on the floor. Then he began to vomit and lost control of his bladder and bowels. On top of everything else, a wild Florida thunderstorm blew up and started dumping rain on the car. "Brute hates thunder and lightning," said Fran. "He began to cry. It was terrible. The rain was coming down so hard I couldn't see, and yet I was driving like a maniac to save my dog." She drove with one hand on the wheel, her other hand trying to keep Brute's head up so he could breathe.

Arriving at the clinic, Fran carried the dog inside. She immediately got bad news. The veterinary clinic had no way to treat a coral snakebite. The only treatment was administration of an antivenin called *M. fulvius*, which the clinic didn't have. The antivenin is very rare because it's so rarely needed. Of the 15,000 pets bitten by snakes each year in the United States, only one percent are bitten by coral snakes. Most of the bitten animals suffer less venomous strikes and recover on their own. But because of the severity of Brute's bite, he needed the antivenin—now.

The vet staff suggested Fran rush him to Miami or even Gainesville, where there might be a better chance of securing the medicine.

"He's not going to make it to Gainesville," Fran insisted. "That's three-and-a-half hours away!"

The staff took Brute to an examining room. Fran paced the floor, waiting and worrying. The vet came out and tried to prepare Fran for what was likely to happen. They could make him comfortable with an IV and some medication, but there was no other treatment they could offer. To make matters worse, once the symptoms began they usually progressed rapidly and were very difficult to reverse.

The staff called the animal clinics in Gainesville and Miami to locate vials of antivenin, but they soon gave up. They had other emergencies to deal with and no one seemed to have the antidote. By this time, Fran was distraught and crying. She was asked if she wanted Brute put down. Fran refused. "Give me the phone book. I'll make more calls," she said. She started cold calling clinics, hospitals, and anyplace that might have antivenin. Six calls. Six times she heard, "No, we don't have any coral snake antivenin."

"Then I remembered something I'd been told a hundred million times before in my life," said Fran. "'You need to let go and let God handle it. You need to stop your frantic running around in circles and ask for God's help.'"

Fran, always the caretaker, always the one who refused to quit or admit failure, finally stopped and prayed. "Okay, fine," she said silently to God, her heart aching. "I am defeated. God, I need Your help. Please help me. Please help Brute!"

She held her breath, and punched in the number for the next hospital on her list. Registered Nurse Gene Piche answered. Fran told Gene about what had happened to Brute, and the story resonated with the nurse. Gene told her how much he loved his own dog, a German shepherd. Then he called the pharmacy at his hospital and found what Fran was looking for. The hospital had seven vials of antivenin. Two of the vials were set to expire, and the hospital agreed to sell those.

The price was astronomical though—up in the four-figure range. "The bill was ridiculous," said Fran. "Afterward I got flak from some people, but they didn't understand that Brute is a family member."

By now it was three hours since the bite. Within half an hour the antivenin had been delivered and administered, but Brute still wasn't doing well. His red blood count was falling and his kidneys were shutting down. "It was a struggle," Fran shared. "They had to ice him down. His whole neurological system went, and they told me he probably wasn't going to make it."

They asked Fran to leave the treatment area to make room for other emergencies, but she refused. They put Brute in a comfortable, floor-level animal cage. Fran sat next to him. "I didn't want him to think he was being punished or abandoned," she later told a reporter for the *St. Petersburg Times*.

Late that night, things began to look up. Brute stabilized enough for Fran to go home for a few hours of sleep. But in the middle of the night the clinic called. Brute had taken a turn for the worse, his red blood cell count dropping to dangerous levels. Fran raced back and stayed as the vets injected more antivenin. The next day, the dog needed a blood transfusion.

Fran enlisted her family, friends, and people at her church to pray for Brute. She wouldn't give up her dog without a fight. She enlisted everyone she knew to pray.

And then Brute turned a corner. Within three days he was eating his favorite treat: French-style hamburger rolls from Publix grocery store. A couple days later Brute went home. The news got out, and Brute's convalescence became a community-wide event. "He had lots of people pulling for him," said Fran. Then the media got involved. The story of Brute's bravery raced around the world.

"I got emails and calls from all over," Fran shared. "I was touched by the people who wanted to help. One crippled lady in a wheelchair, who didn't have a job, sent me $5. I sent it back and suggested she donate it to a golden retriever rescue group."

The experience had an impact on Fran's family too. If Brute hadn't seen the snake and acted as quickly as he did, the events of that day might have been very different. "I think it proved to my grandchildren that the animals we are responsible for also feel responsible for us. I also hope they learned that pets are an important part of our family. They get the same treatment as any other family member. And I think everyone around me realizes the commitment it takes to properly care for animals."

The year following the snakebite, Fran got an enexpected phone call. Brute had won the National Hero Dog Award from the Society for the Prevention of Cruelty to Animals (SPCA). They wanted Fran and Brute to fly out to accept it. Fran thought it was a joke at first, but Brute's heroic feat beat out 200 other dogs for the award.

"A lot of dogs might have just barked or run away. But Brute went for the snake and took the bite,"[1] said Madeline Bernstein, president of the Lost Angeles chapter of the SPCA, which selects an annual Hero Dog and then nominates it for the national award.

Brute did recover from the coral snakebite, but he was never quite as strong and lively. "It took a toll on him," Fran said. "But he still followed me around. He still liked his bath. He still liked to ride in the car. He was still afraid of thunder and lightning. And he still liked to have his back scratched. I hovered over him, watching him closely and checking his gums constantly to see if they were pink and the blood was circulating," Fran admitted.

"He was such a sissy boy," her husband Mark still teases. "He was always pulling on your apron strings."

Fran didn't care. There was a bond between them, forged on a rainy autumn evening when Brute saved her grandkids from a deadly snake and his life hung on a phone call, a prayer, and a tiny vial of antivenin.

Fran raised Brute from a pup. She was there when he was born and helped deliver him. But when she first saw the tiny golden retriever pup, she noticed something strange. "He came out in a green amniotic sack. I had never seen anything like it. I thought, 'What is this?'" At first she thought of naming him Kermit, but that didn't seem to fit such a big, beautiful puppy. She caught herself exclaiming, "He looks like a brute!" It was the perfect name for a golden retriever who would someday tip the scales at 125 pounds. His full name was Brutis Maximus, inspired by the Maximus character in the Academy Award-winning Russell Crowe film *Gladiator*. When I talked to Fran recently by phone, she had several dogs in her office, including a new one she'd just adopted. The big, unruly puppy jumped on her lap as we spoke, and she had to shoo him off. There will always be dogs in Fran's lap, but there will never be another Brute.

4

Faith on Two Feet

*Now faith is the substance of things hoped for,
the evidence of things not seen.*

Hebrews 11:1 nkjv

Faith is believing when common sense tells you not to."[1] Faith is also the name of a smiling yellow dog who walks on two legs. You can see her, but it's still hard to believe. Faith walks!

Jude Stringfellow was a single mom with three kids when her son Reuben came home one day with a suspicious bundle tucked into his number 63 football jersey. "He walked right into the kitchen and wouldn't stop smiling," Jude said. "I knew something was up."

The bundle began to move, and Reuben couldn't stop smiling. He untangled his jersey, and there was a tiny yellow puppy with a very strange looking body.

Reuben had been out with his best friend whose dog, Princess, had recently given birth to a litter of puppies. He had called Reuben to help because for some reason several of the puppies were either dead or dying. Jude overheard the conversation and had an inkling of what Reuben just might have in mind. She told him straight up, "Reuben, you cannot bring a dog home. You *cannot* bring a puppy home, do you hear me?"

The Stringfellow family, including Jude, "are all marshmallow-hearted," she said. "We fall for any animal, sick or healthy. We are always fostering, rescuing, and caring for animals one way or the other." And Reuben, although a 17-year-old boy, was no different.

When they first found the dogs, Reuben and his friend came upon a nightmarish scene. Princess was a junkyard guard dog, not a pet, and she had given birth to a litter of sick and deformed puppies that were unable to suckle. The puppies appeared dead, and the two boys were passing the dead puppies through a fence to dispose of them when Reuben heard something whimpering and scratching. There was one tiny puppy alive. They watched in horror as Princess repeatedly covered the puppy, with her body, then stood up and looked down at it. For some reason the mother dog was trying to suffocate the last little puppy, and it was just barely alive. Reuben didn't hesitate; he pushed Princess aside with his foot, scooped up the struggling puppy, wrapped her in his shirt, and took her home to his mother. Reuben noticed the puppy was missing a front leg.

Back in the kitchen, the puppy's tiny body fit into Reuben's hand. She lay there silently, looking straight into Jude's eyes. "I couldn't stop staring at her face," Jude said. "I prayed and I asked God to make her live. I cried, and I took her from Reuben's hand." Weak and starving, the puppy was probably just a few weeks old. Her fur was matted with filth. Even worse, she was missing her right foreleg and her left foreleg looked grossly deformed. "It pointed backward and was upside down," said Jude. In addition, there was no joint where the elbow should be and the paw had seven toes.

Just like the little pup's body, Jude's feelings were tangled and complicated. *What if she doesn't live? I don't know if I want to get attached to her. How could Reuben do this to me? He knows the landlord said "No dogs." And the girls have already lost so many pets. It will be so hard on them if this puppy doesn't survive.*

While Jude looked, trying to decide what to do, the puppy opened her mouth and tried to cry, but no sound came out. "She had a look of desire in her eyes," said Jude. "She wanted to be helped. She wanted to be cared for. She seemed to be asking for us to help her." Jude knew the puppy was starving, dehydrated, and near death. There was no way she was going to let her die.

But even if she survived, Jude wasn't quite sure what this dog's life would be like. Her mind started reeling again. Would she ever be able to walk? Or go outside? Would she ever get to play with other dogs? And how would she get around to eat or to relieve herself?

Before she even attempted a feeding, Jude decided to bathe the puppy and remove the matted dirt and filth. She washed her in the kitchen sink, and it took several attempts to get her clean. As her pretty golden fur began to emerge from layers of muck, the puppy began to suck at Jude's fingers. She was hungry; that was a good sign. Jude mixed up some baby formula and gave the puppy a tiny drop. She acted excited and drank a little bit more, awkwardly licking up the fluid.

The puppy survived the night. The next morning Jude whisked her off to the vet's office for a professional opinion. The vet, a childhood friend of Jude's, was not optimistic. She said it would be very difficult for the puppy to ever learn to walk, and in her career she had never seen a dog without the use of both front legs. They both noticed the puppy moved by throwing herself down on her face, then pulling her head back quickly and scooting her body an inch or two forward, before throwing herself down on her face again. The vet explained that if the puppy continued to scoot around like this she would probably do permanent damage to her chest and her chin.

What will we do? Jude wondered. *Maybe we can find a way to get her to sit up or even hop like a rabbit.* But that was still in the future. For now, they needed to keep the puppy alive.

Jude, Reuben, and his two sisters, Laura and Caity, set the alarm clock to go off every two hours. Jude got up first and fed the puppy with an eyedropper. When she went back to bed, she gave the clock to Laura, who got up two hours later. Then Caity took a turn. Last was

Reuben. For the first few weeks, the family worked day and night to feed the puppy every couple of hours, along with giving her lots of love and attention. The family didn't know what to name this little junkyard dog who had invaded their home and taken over their lives. She didn't yet have a real name but went by "Puppy," "Yellow Mutt," and even "Terror." Jude usually just called her "Yellow Dog."

Jude still wanted to get the puppy up so she wasn't falling on her face. They dreamed of training her to walk but didn't know how to go about it because they had never seen a dog walking upright on its hind legs. They formed a plan. First they would try to teach her to sit upright and back on her haunches, like a squirrel. The second goal was to get her to move forward by hopping, almost like a rabbit. They weren't sure if she could do it, but they decided to give it a try.

Dogs do almost anything for food, and the reward that really seemed to grab the puppy's attention was peanut butter on a spoon. Yellow Dog loved peanut butter! When she sat up they rewarded her with a bite. Gummy Bears worked too because they could be thrown.

Weeks and weeks passed with Jude and the kids leading Yellow Dog around the house using peanut butter on a spoon. If she wanted peanut butter, she had to somehow get her chest and chin up in the air. If she scooted around on her chest, she didn't get the reward.

During this period, Yellow Dog's inner determination began to emerge. Jude calls it "doggedness," something that kept the puppy moving onward and upward. One day Laura placed some peanut butter on a paper plate on top of Jude's bed. Yellow Dog wanted the peanut butter but couldn't reach it. She whined and started to make gurgling noises. The smell of peanut butter was driving her crazy.

Jude put a couple of pillows on the floor so Yellow Dog could get closer, but she still couldn't reach it. Jude wasn't teasing the dog. She knew the dog had to learn to figure out how to do some things for herself. Then the dog surprised them. Another family pet, a Welsh Corgi puppy named Ean, climbed up on the pillow with Yellow Dog. The new puppy promptly climbed up on top of him, using him as a step to get to the peanut butter. Then she used her teeth to pull herself the rest of the way on to the bed. She had done it! She made quick work of the peanut butter, and Jude celebrated her accomplishment as the dog proudly surveyed the world from atop the bed.

Eventually Yellow Dog learned to hop. She couldn't move fast, but she could move across the room in big jumps that made everyone laugh. She was officially off the ground and no longer scooting around on her chin. Jude was pleased and satisfied.

One day something strange happened. On Reuben's eighteenth birthday the family was outside with Yellow Dog and Ean. The two dogs were inseparable, fighting and playing all day long. Before the birthday celebration, Jude had stopped at the grocery store for big, meaty bones for the dogs to enjoy. Each dog got a bone, but Ean got greedy, dropped his, and came running straight at Yellow Dog. He knocked her over, bit her leg, and stole her bone. Ean ran away with it, looking back to see her reaction. All of a sudden Yellow Dog jumped upright, landed on her feet, and began to run, one foot in front of the other. She went into overdrive and moved faster than any dog Jude had ever seen. Yellow Dog stretched herself upright, grabbed Ean by the neck, and shook him. He dropped her bone. Yellow Dog picked it up and walked back to her spot, unruffled. She loved Ean, but a bone was a bone.

After that, Yellow Dog got a new name. The deformed, dying pup they had rescued would now be called "Faith" because that was the only way they could explain what they had seen. This dog was a miracle, and she walked by faith.

"At the time Faith came into my life—our lives—we were just getting over a terrible family situation," Jude explained. A nasty divorce had shaken the family and brought financial difficulties and emotional challenges. "There was hurt and heartache lingering around our daily lives." Jude and her three kids had to find a way to climb out of the pit and create a new and better life. Faith arrived at just the right moment to lead the way.

"Thank God for Faith," said Jude. "It gave us a chance as a family to forget about our problems and concentrate on her…Her situation reminded me of the fact that I had pretty bad problems going on in my family, and I wasn't able to completely overcome any of them by myself either." By throwing herself into rehabilitating Faith, nursing her to good health, and training her to hop and then to walk, Jude could, like Faith, rise upright and climb out of her own painful situation.

Faith changed Jude's life and the lives of her children. And she is still changing the lives of people around the world. After Faith learned how to walk, the news media became interested. Faith first appeared on a local news program in Oklahoma City. When the cameraman came to the house to shoot some footage for the feel-good story about overcoming obstacles, he was shocked to see Faith walk toward him. Somehow the personnel at the station thought this would be a cute little pet trick, like a circus dog who can hop upright for a few feet to get a food treat. But when Faith stood up and walked "like a human," the story took on a whole new slant. He ended up filming Faith walking across the yard, up some stairs, over the curb, and around the neighborhood. Occasionally she hopped, skipped, and jumped too.

Jude's daughter Laura handled the interview and revealed the real reason why Faith could walk. She told the interviewer that it was due to God. KFOR-TV aired the interview and the footage. Linda Cavanaugh, the station anchor, said, "Sometimes these stories leave you scratching your head in wonder." The next day, reporters from all over the world called Jude. Faith's story was picked up by the Associated Press, and Faith was featured on many media shows, including Keith Olbermann's *MSNBC Countdown, Ripley's Believe It or Not, Inside Edition, Entertainment Tonight, Ricki Lake, Maury Povich, Montel Williams,* and *The Oprah Winfrey Show.* Even the *National Enquirer* was interested.

Faith was awarded celebrity status by several airlines, so she gets to ride in a seat, strapped in just like human passengers. When she flies, Faith draws a lot of attention. She usually sits quietly or sleeps, but sometimes she's allowed to walk around the front of the cabin to meet people and accept treats. She loves it when people laugh. "It perks her ears a bit, and she opens that mouth and begins to smile," Jude shared.

Faith also makes appearances on military bases, in hospitals, and at churches. Although the two-legged dog changed their lives and showed the Stringfellows they could survive anything, Jude believes Faith was created for something even more important: to help people, especially children, in need. "She helps us all understand we can do anything we set our hearts and minds to," said Jude. "We take that message around the world with her."

In many ways, Faith is unique. Yet she still is a normal dog. When she was just a few months old, Jude was taking her for a walk in Dolese Park when a squirrel suddenly came running out of a tunnel on the playground. The squirrel stopped and stared at Faith. Perhaps it was the creature's standard fear of dogs, but it might also have been startled at the sight of a two-legged dog standing upright. Before Jude realized what was going to happen, Faith took off after the squirrel! She chased it through the woods, over a low-hanging wire, and up a tree. Faith stood at the bottom of the tree staring up at the squirrel. Her pursuit had taken her more than a hundred yards at a full run.

"She hopped straight up several times trying to reach him," Jude said, but she couldn't quite figure out how to climb the tree. "I was so proud of Faith. I told her that she was just as normal as any other dog I'd ever met."

"Faith, the Two-Legged Dog" is now a trademark, and Faith's story has reached millions around the world. A day in the life of Faith, however, is mostly like that of any other dog. It revolves around eating, sleeping, and going outside to go to the bathroom. Faith prefers to sleep under a bed where she likes to shred the mattress lining and gnaw on the baseboards. She also likes to watch a little TV and take walks around the neighborhood. But when Jude calls, "Let's go, Dog!"—and especially if there is luggage involved—Faith comes out ready to roll.

If you'd like to see photos or read more about Faith, go to http://faiththedog.info. Here's a snippet from a book Jude wrote about her unique dog, *With a Little Faith:*

Faith is the evidence of things not seen. Can you see it? Take a walk with me someday…when you do, watch the people as they see the laughing little yellow dog. They lose something when they do. They lose their fear of the day, they lose their burdens…for them this moment is all there is.

5

Freddie Takes Flight

~≈~

Survival is triumph enough.

HARRY CREWS

Freddie was a bit of a grump. "He always considered himself the alpha male regardless of how many other dogs were around," said Jill Doran, matriarch of the Slevin family. The Pekingese mix was full of chutzpah and loved to throw his weight around, even though it amounted to just 15 pounds.

Jill's family rescued Freddie back when they lived in New Jersey. His owner had died, and he ended up at the humane society. At 11 years old he was considered unadoptable, but Jill has always taken in abandoned animals, especially those that aren't prime adoption material. Over the years she's rescued many different breeds of dogs. She's had Pekingese mixes before, but Freddie was the most "Peke" of them all with his flat face, pointy ears, and upturned nose. "He had huge feet—kind of like basset hound feet," Jill said.

Although he sometimes acted like a grumpy old man, Freddie

made Jill and her family laugh. As he aged, he lost a number of teeth and began to wake up from naps with his tongue hanging out "because his teeth weren't holding it in," said Jill. "We'd be looking over at him and there he was, sticking his tongue out at us."

The Pekingese breed originated in China, where they were kept as pampered pets in the Chinese Imperial Court. The Chinese thought they resembled Chinese guardian lions, and so they went by the name "Lion Dog." They were also called "Sleeve Pekingese" because they were often tucked into the sleeves of robes worn by Chinese royalty. A 2000-year-old breed, Pekingese dogs have a distinctive flat face and bowed legs. A set of instructions for breeding Pekingese dogs from Chinese Empress Dowager Cixi includes:

> Let it be lively that it may afford entertainment by its gambols; let it be timid that it may not involve itself in danger; let it be domestic in its habits that it may live in amity with the other beasts, fishes or birds that find protection in the Imperial Palace.

Somehow Freddie missed the imperial memo on living in "amity." Over the years, instead of mellowing, Freddie got crankier. "He definitely had an attitude," Jill said. "Early on he would stand his ground and bark and snap" if anyone tried to pick him up or approach him unexpectedly. Later on he grew more temperamental as his eyesight and hearing began to fail. "But he always got along with females," Jill said. "Any females—large or small—he liked. And he always got along with smaller animals.

But with bigger dogs, it was a different story. "We have two big Labrador retriever mixes," said Jill. "Freddie got into tussles with them a few times and didn't come out on the good side because he was 15 pounds and they were 65."

Freddie's feisty personality probably saved him one cold winter's day when he had the fight of his life against something much more lethal than a Labrador.

The Peke had lived with them for just a year when Jill and her family relocated to a seven-acre property below the Bridger Foothills in Bozeman, Montana. Bozeman is a city of about 30,000 people at the foot of the Bridger Mountains, a sub range of the Rocky Mountains that stretches 3000 miles from British Columbia, Canada, to New Mexico. Louis and Clark traveled through the Bozeman area in 1806 with Sacajawea as a guide. Sacajawea Peak, 9665 feet high, is a prominent mountain visible from Bozeman. A gorgeous and rugged area, Bozeman is familiar to many people as a film location in Robert Redford's films *A River Runs Through It* and *The Horse Whisperer.*

The mountains and hills are home to a wide array of wildlife, including foxes, coyote, pheasants, deer, and the occasional black or grizzly bear. Since she was new to living in such a rugged area, Jill wasn't too familiar with every facet of Montana wildlife. She did know how much the dogs enjoyed roaming their acreage and exploring the quiet neighborhood, a subdivision made up of properties ranging from 2 to 20 acres in size.

Freddie and Balto, one of the family's other dogs, had established a daily routine of trotting over to a neighbor's house for a visit. The neighbor was a friend of the Slevin family and, like Jill, she volunteered at the local Humane Society. She enjoyed having the dogs visit, and Jill suspected she even lured the dogs over with hot dogs and other treats.

On December 29, the two dogs went out for their afternoon walk to the neighbors, but only one dog came back. Balto returned but Freddie did not. Jill was immediately concerned. Freddie had never run away before. Pekingese dogs are not good outdoor dogs and can be especially sensitive to hot and cold temperatures. The average temperatures this time of year in that part of Montana range from 33 degrees during the day to 14 degrees at night. There was also some snow on the ground. In addition, Freddie was an old dog. Jill felt they should act fast to get him back into the warm house.

It was around four in the afternoon when the family mobilized to search the neighborhood. With his short legs he couldn't have gotten very far, they figured. They walked around their neighborhood, looking and calling for Freddie. The neighborhood kids and some adults who were visiting friends for the holidays jumped in and helped too. But Freddie was nowhere to be found. The family stayed up late and got up before dawn to start the search again.

Freddie did have a long coat of fur, so Jill felt they had a good chance of finding him alive, but she also knew he was probably suffering from the cold. They spent the next week searching. They downloaded instructions from the Internet on how to find lost dogs and followed them to the letter. They contacted the sheriff's department and the road department to see if there had been any sightings. They put up posters in pet stores and grocery stores. Jill even talked to the local snowplow operator to put him on alert. "If you turn over something that looks like Freddie, call me and I will come!" Jill told him.

Nothing worked. Freddie was still missing. Jill was even pondering how to break it to the children that Freddie might not be coming home.

About a week later, Jill was in her home office at the back of the house when the babysitter came running in. "Jill! Jill! Jill!" she cried. "One of the dogs in the house is barking frantically at the front door!"

Jill jumped up and ran to the door. She opened it and found Freddie. She was horrified. He was covered in icicles, and his eyes were red, swollen, and looked horribly infected. "He just kind of collapsed into the house," Jill said. She grabbed a blanket, wrapped Freddie in it to warm him up, and called the vet. On her first call, she got an answering machine. Then she called the Humane Society for help. "I think they had me on caller ID at that point," said Jill. "They were probably saying 'It's the pathetic lady with the missing dog calling again.'"

The Humane Society told Jill to put the Pekingese on a warming pad and gave her the phone numbers of more veterinarians. The first vet was in surgery and couldn't be reached, but the second vet, John McIlhattan, was available. Jill rushed Freddie down to his office. During the exam, the vet discovered the dog's body temperature was very low, Freddie's eyes were scratched up with some possible damage to the corneas, and his body was covered in a rash from insect bites, although he didn't have any active bugs on him.

What Dr. McIlhattan discovered next shocked Jill. He was looking for wounds and found some very strange gouges across Freddie's shoulders and back. "They looked like talon marks," he said. Jill hadn't noticed the marks under Freddie's fur, and she hadn't seen any blood either.

The veterinarian shaved off the fur around the area for a closer look. He found eight to ten puncture wounds. After measuring the marks, the vet gave his final opinion: "With the size of the talon marks and the location, it looks like this is an eagle grab." He told Jill that it was likely Freddie had been grabbed by a golden eagle multiple times, the talons puncturing and raking across the dog's back, shoulders, and neck.

As a new transplant from the East Coast, Jill didn't know that the Bridger Mountain Range ranks as the number one golden eagle flyway in the United States.[1] Migrating hawks and eagles save energy by drafting upward on the westerly winds along the north–south ridges of the Bridgers. On just one autumn day, up to 250 golden eagles and hawks can be spotted in the annual raptor count conducted by the Montana Audubon Society.

The golden eagle is a massive bird with a wingspan of seven feet. An adult bird weighs from 7 to 13 pounds, but there have been reports of 20-pounders in the northwestern United States. Golden eagles usually prey on rabbits, marmots, ground squirrels, and other birds. But the eagles have also been known to prey on larger mammals such as fox, wild and domestic cats, mountain goats, and even deer.

Golden eagles usually attack their prey using one foot to grab the head of the animal while the talons of the other foot drive into the lungs or other soft parts of the body. An eagle's foot has three curved talons in the front for grabbing and holding and one larger talon in the back that can be used to rake deep gouges into the body of the prey and help it grasp its prey. An eagle's powerful beak isn't usually used during the killing process; its primary use is for tearing prey apart for devouring.

It's impossible to know exactly what happened to Freddie, but the best guess is that Freddie was innocently hanging out at the neighbor's house when a golden eagle, circling high above the foothills, spotted him. Golden eagles have extremely sharp eyesight and can see five to six times better than humans, perfect for sighting prey from great distances. Eagles usually fly from 20 to 60 miles per hour, but they can dive at more than 100 miles per hour when in attack mode. It's possible that the eagle, after zeroing in on Freddie, tucked its wings and went into a high-speed attack dive. Because Freddie survived the initial attack, however, it's more likely the eagle was close by and swooped to get him instead of diving.

After grabbing the dog, the eagle probably tried to carry Freddie to a tree or a rocky point to make a meal of him. Freddie was fighting for his life, growling, kicking, and squirming to get free. Although golden eagles attack large prey, it's difficult for them to carry anything heavier than a few pounds. This eagle obviously was struggling and eventually dropped Freddie. The dog may have gotten the wind knocked out of him and lay motionless, or he tried to run away as fast as his little old-man legs could carry him while dodging the large bird, or perhaps he was looking for a place to hide. Whatever he was doing, the eagle struck again…and again, leaving the deep gouges on Freddie's body.

Eventually the eagle gave up. Eagles fail at killing their intended prey more often than not. According to wildlife experts, golden eagles have a hunting success rate of approximately 30 percent. This time the odds worked in Freddie's favor, expecially when his fighting spirit kicked in.

Eagle attacks on pets aren't unheard of. Not long ago a bald eagle attacked a 13-pound dachshund named Ava in rural Maine. The eagle swooped down, snatched her, and carried her about 300 feet before dropping her. Ava survived but underwent two surgeries—one to combat a nasty infection caused by the talon punctures and the other to repair injuries from the fall.

Another story out of Illinois comes from an avid bird watcher named Eric Walters. He was astonished to observe a golden eagle attack a terrified white tailed deer in a snowy field. His series of photographs tell the story. The eagle first spotted the deer from the air, went into a dive, and then leveled out, flying at high speed toward the deer.

When it caught up to the fleeing deer, the eagle raked its large back talons across the animal's hindquarters, leaving long, deep wounds. The deer changed direction and then began zigzagging. The eagle followed, its eyes locked onto its prey. In an adrenaline-fueled burst of speed, the deer continued to run erratically with the eagle in hot pursuit eight feet above the ground. The eagle had a hard time keeping up with the rapid changes in direction, and after a few moments the raptor gave up and the deer escaped.

Freddie had also escaped, but his ordeal wasn't over. He still had to get back home. After the eagle grab, Freddie probably hid for a while in the foothills. He may have discovered an abandoned animal den in the rocks, which would explain the rash from flea or mite bites. Cold, injured, alone, and hungry, he waited, making sure the eagle was gone and perhaps gathering his strength. During the week Freddie was out in the wilderness, the temperatures dropped to below zero, and the Bozeman area experienced significant snowfall. Somehow Freddie stayed warm enough to survive and eventually made his way to his house. Freddie's canine homing instinct guided him to the front door so Jill could find him. Wounded, starving, and covered in ice, Freddie had made it. He was home. He had survived. The grumpy little Pekingese had battled a golden eagle and won.

It took Freddie a week to recover physically. Jill kept him warm and cozy and let him sleep as much as he wanted. After a few days he went outside but stayed very close to the house. For the rest of his life, Freddie was cautious about going outside, and he seldom ventured beyond the end of the driveway.

The curmudgeonly old Pekingese lived to the ripe old age of 19. And until the end of his life, Freddie still thought of himself as the alpha male. Freddie's amazing survival taught Jill and her kids "the power of the underdog"—that someone so small can triumph against such overwhelming odds.

Jill's family and friends have followed in her footsteps of loving the animal friends God puts in our lives. Many are heavily involved in 4-H, where they raise rabbits, train horses, and help kids learn about caring for animals. Jill's oldest daughter, a lively 15-year-old, is a counselor for a local nonprofit that teaches handicapped and disabled children and adults how to handle and ride horses. Jill's younger children are involved in animal rescue and care, recently helping place an abandoned goat in a safe and supportive environment.

And Jill? She still misses Freddie, her "little miracle man." The memory of Freddie's week out in the cold is still just as fresh as when it first happened. There was always a close bond between the two, but after the eagle incident their bond grew even stronger. "He loved curling up on my clothes," she said. "If I took off a pair of jeans at night, in the morning that's where I'd find him curled up." After the eagle ordeal, Freddie was treated like the Chinese royal dog he believed himself to be. He got whatever he wanted to eat. "You want baloney?" Jill would ask him. "Then you get baloney!"

6

Galloping Andre

～✷～

I think dogs are the most amazing creatures;
they give unconditional love. For me they are
the role model for being alive.

Gilda Radner

Karen was having her afternoon cup of tea and a Nutella sandwich when she got a phone call. Living in Wasilla, Alaska, she'd been involved in dog rescues all her life and had lots of stories, but nothing had ever come close to the one she was about to experience. Dennis, an animal control officer, said, "I've got something really horrible, Karen."

Dennis worked in Houston, Alaska, a small town about 14 miles away from where Karen lived. She caught her breath, said, "Okay," and waited.

"I've got this dog here, and two of his legs are missing. I don't know what to do with him. He's emaciated. I've never seen anything like this," Dennis responded.

Karen's heart began to pound. It always did when a dog's life was on the line. "Oh, quickly get him to the vet," she instructed. Karen works for Alaska Dog and Puppy Rescue, and her job is to help coordinate medical care for stray or roaming dogs. She'd been with the group for about seven years. She usually got calls from veterinarians and animal control when they dealt with a dog that was sick or injured and they didn't know who the owner was. Karen has access to some medical funds to help the dogs that don't have anyone to care about them.

Although she didn't yet know the details, Karen was anxious. That particular animal control office didn't have much in the way of funds to pay for veterinary care, so her role was crucial for this dog's survival, whatever his condition was. And it was so much worse than she imagined.

"You've never seen anything like this, Karen," said the vet when she called to give her an update. "He's missing two of his legs. I think he's been in a snare." She went on to explain that each leg had been severed above the knee joint, leaving two stumps.

Karen's thoughts immediately went to the debate that was raging about the use of animal traps. The controversy was prominent in the local media. About half of the Alaskan population was against the use of brutal traps that were used to snare wolves and wolverines. The other half was for it. And one thing was certain—the traps were catching dogs along with the intended prey. The traps were barbaric devices. They were metal, spring-loaded, and had sharp teeth, like something from a medieval torture dungeon. They're still sold online. One advertisement hawking traps for Alaskan wolves states, "[This trap] is much too strong for the Lower 48 states." Karen shuddered as she imagined what the dog had been through. But she didn't yet know the worst.

"He's ugly and emaciated," the vet continued. "Looking at his wounds, it looks like this happened two or three weeks ago. Karen, one leg bone was probably snapped in the snare, but the dog chewed the skin of that leg and completely through the other leg to escape the trap."

Karen sat back, stunned. Her head spun and she felt dizzy. The vet went on as Karen listened in shock. The dog was very near death. "Well, what can we do for him?" Karen asked, her voice thin and shaky.

The vet took her time answering, weighing the options. Finally, she responded, "I feel bad putting him to sleep after he's survived several weeks on his own with these wounds and in this condition. I just can't do that. But I can't say he's going to live either."

Karen jumped in her car and rushed over. She burst into the vet's office. There he was, lying on an examining table. He wagged his tail when he saw her, but he was too weak to lift his head. He was a big dog—maybe a Rottweiler-shepherd mix. When healthy, he would probably weigh between 85 and 90 pounds. Currently he was down to 40.

Karen wasn't sure what to do, but she had a reputation of never giving up on anyone or anything. "My friends also know I'm a little bit cuckoo," she says. When she arrived, she and the vet looked at each other. "I can't let him die," Karen said. "I don't want him put to sleep. Why don't I just pick him up and take him to my house? If he's going to die, at least it will be on a warm bed, his head in someone's lap, and knowing he is loved." She cried quietly as she got the words out.

The vet pumped the injured dog full of fluids and antibiotics. They had no idea how he would be able to get around because he was missing two legs on the same side or even if he would survive the night. "Let's deal with how he'll walk when we get to it," the vet said. "Frankly I don't think he's going to live."

Karen put the dog on the backseat of her car. "I'm going to take him home and see what happens," she told the vet.

Once he was at Karen's home, she went to work. Although the animal was starving, every time he managed to eat some food it came right back up again. Being so close to death, his body had already started to shut down and his internal organs were barely functioning. Karen coaxed some teeny bits of chicken into him, along with some rice, broth, and yogurt, but he still couldn't keep much down. He had terrible diarrhea that the vet had determined was from giardia, a virulent microorganism contracted from drinking dirty water.

As the dog lay quietly, warm and drowsy in Karen's little kitchen, she got the chance to examine his wounds more closely. The front left leg was a very clean wound, just like a knife had sliced through it. It was probably severed when the trap snapped shut. The back left leg was a different story, more like a jagged wound with bone sticking out. That was the leg he had chewed off to escape. It looked pretty clean, all things considered. He'd licked it, and the cold had probably helped stem the bleeding. The dog was warm and safe for the moment.

Karen eventually got the full story from Dennis. Animal control had received a call from a lady in town who had seen a dog crawling across a road, leaving a trail of blood. The weather was horrific. It was February and about 20 degrees below zero. The officers went out there, found the trail of blood, and tracked the dog to an old camper shell on the ground. He was hiding underneath and growled when they tried to get him out. It was dark and cold, so they decided to come back the following morning. They figured he'd probably be dead and that would solve their problem.

But he wasn't. The next morning Dennis went out with a couple of other people to check on the dog. They were stunned to find him still under the camper shell and alive. They dragged him out, and that's when Karen got the first call.

Karen shuddered. *How did this dog survive?* Besides his horrific injuries and massive loss of blood, he'd probably been in shock and without food and fresh water. *He's a fighter, this one.*

A few weeks passed, and the dog's perilous and painful ordeal was just a memory, but he had a long journey ahead. A very long journey. Karen had to carry him everywhere. For three months, he spent the days and nights on a blanket next to her kitchen table. She picked him up and carried him outside five or six times a day to go to the bathroom. While he relieved himself, she literally held him up because he couldn't stand on his two remaining legs.

Karen's vet, an experienced surgeon she trusted to let her know if a dog should be put to sleep or not, was appalled at the dog's condition. "Oh, boy," was all he said, sighing the first time he saw the dog. But after an examination and observing the dog's wagging tail and alert ears that rotated as he tracked their conversation, the vet advised, "Don't give up on him, Karen."

"That's all I needed to hear," she said. "I won't give up. But how's he going to walk? How's he going to get around?"

"He'll figure it out," the vet said. "He's got that personality that always wants to try. He'll figure it out."

Karen's friends were used to her animal-loving ways and her stubborn persistence, but even they questioned the enormous amount of time and energy she was pouring into the mutilated dog. "Karen, what are you doing?" some of her closest friends asked. "This isn't fair to the dog. This is inhumane and even cruel."

"I don't see any bad in anything," Karen admitted. "I'm just a little off the deep end sometimes. There were days when I would look at him and say, 'Am I helping you? Or is this just me refusing to give up on you?'" One day when she was dressing his wounds she looked into his eyes. "Am I just trying to prove something to myself?" she asked. "You just have to let me know if you want to stop trying, boy, and I will take you to the vet and let you go."

But when she got up in the morning and saw him wag his tail or when he greeted her with his friendly face and alert eyes and ears when she got home from work, she knew she was doing the right thing. *I can't give up on him.* That became her mantra.

Caring for the dog became a family affair. Karen's husband was from Germany and used to driving at high speeds on the Autobahn. That came in handy on the more than one occasion when he raced the dog to the vet when the critter seemed on the verge of death. Karen's mother-in-law took care of the dog while Karen was gone, and Karen's young daughter loved to read him stories, sitting with him day in and day out. The other family dogs loved him too. They accepted him and often nurtured him by licking his injured legs. The family decided to name him Andre.

After a few weeks of carrying him and holding him up when he needed to go outside, Karen decided there must be a better way. She experimented with duct tape, using huge amounts of padding and veterinary wrap to create a fake extension to his front leg. It didn't work well, but it was a start.

The dog's stumps were healing, and eventually he tried to balance himself in the snow. One day, to Karen's surprise, he tried to run—and almost was successful. As she watched, he tried again and again.

She noticed that if he picked up speed and got his momentum going, he could gallop along a few steps here and there. "It was like riding a bicycle—if you stop, you're going to fall over," she said. "He would always sit and lean on me to rest for a bit, and then he would start again, moving those two injured legs like they still had feet on them."

Karen realized that Andre still had the will to run, but he needed help. One night she sat down at the computer and did a search. She came up with Orthopets, a company that develops technology to help people regain mobility and adapts it to give animals a second chance to enjoy life too.

Orthopets was founded by Martin Kaufmann, who had a background in human prosthetics and orthotics. Martin had a cousin whose dog suffered a stroke and lost the use of a front leg. When the vet recommended amputation, Martin decided there had to be a better way. After trial and error, he came up with a solution that worked and realized that by combining what he knew about human prosthetics and orthotics with the latest technology and research in bracing and adaptive solutions, he could make a significant contribution to the health and happiness of pets across the world. And Orthopets was born.

After Karen contacted them, Orthopets sent up a mold kit that would allow the company to make custom limbs to replace Andre's two left legs. But the cost was going to be about $1000, much more than Karen could afford. "By then Alaska Dog and Puppy Rescue had already spent quite a bit of money on his care, and we couldn't take money away from the other dogs who still needed help. So a lot of his care and expenses became my personal project. I was buying everything for him with my own money."

Six months had passed and Andre was still healing. Karen continued to change his dressings twice a day and put medication on his wounds. He was regaining strength, and his warm and friendly personality emerged. Because she was originally from England, Karen loved to drink tea, and she introduced Andre to her afternoon ritual. Every day she had tea and Nutella sandwiches on squishy white bread, and she soon found out that Andre enjoyed tea and sandwiches too.

One day Andre disappeared from the kitchen, and Karen found him outside with her rabbits. At first she was alarmed and thought he was going to kill them, but she soon realized she should have known better. "He actually loved the rabbits," she said. "He began going out each day to lie down with them. We ended up putting his dog bed out there. The rabbits would look at him through the cage, and pretty soon he was licking the rabbits, washing them."

To raise money for the Orthopets prosthetic limbs, Karen decided to have a garage sale fund-raiser. She went to the local radio station with Andre to make a public announcement. Andre hammed it up, barking into the mic. The radio announcer observed on the air that Andre was drinking tea and eating Nutella sandwiches.

On the day of the garage sale, hundreds of people came by. No one bought anything, but between the children bearing coins and little ladies bearing envelopes, the donations came rolling in. Although mostly one and five dollar bills, enough money was raised to make the casts of Andre's legs and order the prosthetic limbs.

At first the limbs didn't work. Andre had to travel to Colorado to visit Orthopets in person for a custom fitting. This time the process was successful. Andre was fitted with custom hypoallergenic, foam-lined legs specially constructed to fit his stumps. Soon he was playing and doing everything like a normal dog.

As Andre became accustomed to his prosthetics, it soon became apparent that Alaska wasn't a good place for him. The snow packed into his artificial limbs, and the ice was too slippery for him to maneuver well. "It just wasn't the right place for him for the rest of his life," Karen said. "He deserved better." Andre was adopted by a young man down in the Lower 48, and today the dog is thriving.

Karen has been a volunteer for many years at the Alaska Dog and Puppy Rescue in Wasilla, Alaska. She believes she is meant to rescue dogs—but not keep them. "For every animal I keep, that's one less I can rescue. I'm just that stepping-stone that gets them where they're meant to be."

Although Andre no longer lives with her, Karen will never forget the two-legged dog who sat with her for afternoon tea. "Andre became a huge part of our lives and holds a special place in the hearts of the people of Alaska," she said. "It's a true story of never giving up and never thinking something is impossible. He was a mangy, emaciated dog that chewed his own leg off in order to survive. And he did!"

Andre didn't give up, and neither did Karen. "You never know what is possible," she says.

7

Hunter the Brave

Even the tiniest Poodle or Chihuahua
is still a wolf at heart.

DOROTHY HINSHAW PATENT

H unter was just a Chihuahua who had gone through a horren-
dous experience. But he didn't let that slow him down or make
him afraid. He still had the guts to get out into the field with the cattle and herd them around, barking and nipping at their heels to get
them to move.

A full-grown cow can weigh 1000 pounds. Hunter weighed 4. But
it wasn't the moxie the little Chihuahua showed when he ran after the
cattle—any one of them could have deliberately stepped on him at any
moment and ended the chase—and moved them around the field that
reflected his giant-sized heart. No, this little dog named Hunter had recently survived a deadly rollover car accident. He'd escaped from the vehicle and then spent almost two weeks alone out in the elements with no
food or water. During the ordeal he lost half his body weight.

After he survived that wreck, Hunter started playing cattle dog, herding the large mammals around the field.

"He doesn't realize how small he is," said Nannette Haupt, Hunter's owner.

Hunter is a big name for a small dog, but it fits this little Chihuahua. He's orange, just like the Taco Bell dog. He has big, pointy bat ears, and his paws are tipped in white fur. His front half is big and furry and his back end is small and slender. "I call him Little Buff Man because he's built like a body builder," Nannette admitted.

Hunter was a Christmas gift from her mother five years ago when Nannette's husband, Army Staff Sergeant Ryan Haupt, was deployed to Iraq. Less than a year later, on what was supposed to be his last day in Iraq, Ryan was killed. Trained as a sniper, he was part of a special operations group escorting some trucks in the middle of the day. They were attacked by a high-powered, Iranian-made improvised explosive device (IED) near Baqubah, Iraq. The IED is a weapon of choice for insurgent groups in Afghanistan and Iraq. In the U.S. coalition-led war in Iraq, they were responsible for up to 60 percent of coalition soldiers' deaths.[1] IEDS are usually camouflaged and hard to detect. They're also difficult to defend against. "You never know when it's coming," Army SPC Bradley Parrish said in a PBS interview.

This tragedy made Hunter an even more important part of the family, helping Nannette and her parents, Joe and Jane Byrne, grieve. Hunter was very protective of the women in the family. If anyone approached Nannette or Jane too quickly or in a manner that looked threatening to the Chihuahua, he growled, barked, and stood his ground in front of the women. "He's pretty macho," Nannette observed.

Chihuahuas are the smallest known breed of dog, but they have big personalities. The breed originated in Mexico from the *Techichi,* a companion dog developed by the Toltecs. The Aztecs, who conquered the Toltecs, believed the Chihuahuas had mystical powers. They are described as graceful, alert, and fiercely loyal and protective. Hunter lived up to his reputation as the protector of the females in his family.

Then a second tragedy rocked the family. Nanette and her parents packed up their three Chihuahuas, including Hunter, and drove from their home in Colorado Springs to Chicago for a special memorial at Ryan's graveside on his birthday, June 6. Afterward, on the way home, Joe drove through most of the night in their Lincoln Aviator SUV. They stopped along the road in Nebraska to browse some yard sales and accumulated a carload of bargains. About midday, they stopped to switch drivers at the Colorado border, and Jane took the wheel. After driving less than an hour, she fell asleep. The SUV swerved off the highway near a golf course in Sterling, rolling four or five times down a hill.

When the Aviator came to a rest upright, every piece of glass in the vehicle was broken. Joe was banged up but had no serious injuries. Nannette had a broken knee, torn ligaments, and was unconscious. Jane was killed. And in the ensuing horror and confusion, with first-response personnel swarming the accident scene and emergency vehicles arriving, the three frightened Chihuahuas took off.

Hours later, with his daughter still in the hospital, Joe returned to the scene of the accident to look for the dogs. With permission from the sheriff's department to be at the crime scene, Joe and two women from the local Humane Society scoured the area all afternoon. It was hot—the temperature about 95 degrees. They kept searching into the evening looking for any sign of Hunter, Savannah, and Angelina. "I walked for miles and miles around that golf course," Joe said. He also checked the surrounding corn and soybean fields. He found nothing.

As evening drew near, it began to drizzle. With no signs of the dogs, Joe decided to go back up to the highway and retrace the route the SUV had taken when it plunged off the highway. Then he saw her! Savannah, a white Chihuahua with black patches "like a milk cow" was sitting by the highway "like she was waiting for a bus." She was at the exact spot where the SUV went off the road. She was a little skittish, but she finally came when Joe called.

With his wife gone and his daughter still in the hospital, finding Savannah was a small-but-bright spot in an otherwise horrible day.

Joe was not one to sit around, so the very next day he searched for the other two Chihuahuas. He was a man on a mission, and he worked hard to spread the word throughout the community about the two lost dogs. The local radio station made an announcement, and volunteers put up posters that also promised a reward. "Everyone in Sterling knew about the accident," Nannette said.

For the next ten days Joe and Nannette stayed in the area. Then it was time for Jane's memorial service, which was being held in Chicago, where the family was originally from and where Jane and Joe first met. While in Chicago, Joe received a call on his cell phone from the sheriff's office. A small orange Chihuahua had been found. "Does Hunter have white fur on the tips of his paws?" the woman asked.

"That's him! That's Hunter!" Joe exclaimed.

The woman from the sheriff's department said that a couple of days prior, two little boys had been hunting for golf balls around the golf course near the crash site. Matthew Wheeler, ten years old, had picked up a piece of sagebrush and found a little orange ball of fur underneath it. When the Chihuahua looked up with his big pointy bat ears, Matthew and his friend thought he was a baby fox. They picked Hunter up and finally realized he was a dog. They were very excited. Because of his small size, they thought he was just a puppy. Before the accident, he weighed about eight pounds, but now Hunter was down to four.

Matthew took a liking to the forlorn little dog and wanted to keep him. Hunter was glad to be with people who loved and cared for him. The family, who lived on a nearby ranch, fed the dog well. Matthew gave him lots of attention. Living in the country, they were unaware of the ongoing search for the two Chihuahuas lost in the car crash.

One day Matthew's family discovered the little orange Chihuahua had some unusual skills. They caught him out in the fields with the cattle. He was acting like a little herd dog. He was moving the cattle around the field, showing no fear even though the cows towered over him. The family thought it was hilarious.

Shortly thereafter, when the family was out shopping, Matthew's father heard about the SUV accident and the search for the lost dogs. When he got home, he called the number on the reward poster and reported that Matthew had found one Chihuahua and that they were taking good care of him. When Joe and Nannette got the call in Chicago, they were speechless and then amazed. The good news of Hunter's survival helped carry them through the events and intense emotions surrounding Jane's memorial service. When it was over and all the details finalized, they headed home. They were so excited about picking up Hunter that they drove straight through from Chicago, arriving in Sterling around five o'clock in the morning.

The reunion with Hunter was joyful. "There are no words to describe what I felt," said Joe. "It was a miracle." Joe gave Matthew a $200 reward for finding Hunter.

With Hunter's return, the healing process truly began for father and daughter. Nannette went to a rehabilitation center and worked to get off her crutches and regain her strength. Joe busied himself taking care of the two dogs they'd found and his daughter. They talked about what had happened. "We looked at each other," Joe shared, "and even with the back-to-back tragedies and everything that happened, we decided there are so many people across the world that have it so much worse than we do. We decided to focus and move forward, choosing to be happy for the breaks we have. Every morning I wake up and know that I still have a mission to do. There's still something I've gotta do on this earth," Joe explained. "Getting Hunter back was a huge bonus, and the fact that he made it means he still has a mission to do too."

One unusual story surrounding the accident that Joe remembers came from eyewitness reports by three men who were on the golf course for an early round. They watched as the SUV left the highway and tumbled down the hill, kicking up dust and debris. Out of nowhere the wind kicked up and created something like a whirlwind. The men described it as looking like "a small tornado." The swirling wind picked up leaves and dust and the papers that had blown out the SUV's broken windows and carried them up, high into the sky until they were out of sight. It was a bizarre sight, but when Joe heard the story later it comforted him and he held it close to his heart.

Now that Jane is no longer with them, Hunter has transferred all of his protective urges to Nannette. "When I was still healing from the crash, he rested his paws on my injured leg and barked and snarled at anyone who came near it. He's my little guardian now," she said. "He wasn't like that with me before. He sits in the doorway like a little guard.

"Out of the worst tragedies something good can come," Nanette continued. "We got a second chance with Hunter." They never did find Angelina, the smallest of the three lost Chihuahuas. After a year, Nanette and Joe got a new Chihuahua and named her Aspen. She's dark gray with black patches. "Like a sniper's camouflage," Joe explained.

After her husband's death, Nannette decided to switch careers and went back to school for a master's degree in social work. She's halfway through and is working part-time at Fort Carson with families of fallen soldiers in a program called Survivor Outreach Services (SOS). Working in the military environment and helping people who have experienced something like she did makes her feel closer to Ryan.

Hunter regained his weight and his strength and continues to protect Nannette. He can't find any cattle to herd in the neighborhood, but about a month after the accident he did take on a new challenge. Joe and Nannette had taken Hunter out for a slow walk around the cul-de-sac. Joe was still recovering from his bumps and bruises, and Nannette was hobbling around on crutches. They were out at twilight when Hunter ran a few hundred feet ahead and confronted a deer.

Colorado mule deer are large, an adult standing around 42 inches at the shoulder and weighing between 150 to 300 pounds. Granted, they're not as big as the cattle Hunter liked to herd, but they're probably much more dangerous. Although deer have a peaceful air about them, when in danger they rear up on their hind legs and come down hard, stomping and striking out with their front hooves. The small dog didn't care about any of that. Hunter stood his ground in front of the deer, barking and growling, daring the much larger animal to make a move. The deer didn't run away. Instead it squared its body and reared up to strike the Chihuahua.

Joe looked on in horror. *Hunter had survived out in the wild, but now he was going to be taken down by a deer?* Joe and Nanette were near enough to see what was happening, but with their banged up bodies they were too far to get close enough to intervene. It happened quickly. The deer's hooves struck downward with lightning speed while Hunter continued to bark at the top of his lungs.

Somehow the first strike "missed Hunter by a half inch," Joe shared. Nannette and Joe hurried forward as fast as they could. Hunter continued to stand his ground, and the deer lashed out again but missed the little guard dog. Finally, when the humans got close enough, the showdown ended. Joe grabbed Hunter and the deer turned around and ran into the brush.

It was a close call, especially for two people still reeling from such great losses. Hunter's survival reinforced the feeling that he is a very special dog. "I believe in a higher power," said Joe. "You don't get everything back that you lost, but you get some pieces. Same thing with the dogs. You're not going to get all three of them back, but here are two."

Hunter is a tiny little dog with a big job; he serves as a living link to a beloved husband and a cherished wife and mother. Hopefully he won't encounter any more cattle or deer.

A day after the deadly accident, Joe went to the auto salvage yard to go through the SUV. As he sorted through the jumble of belongings, he came across a Sony camera. He was sure it was the camera Nannette had taken to Chicago so he set it aside.

When he took the camera home and presented it to Nannette, she was shocked. "I thought it was gone!" she shrieked. Two years prior, before Ryan had died, Nannette had lost her camera. She'd been upset and looked everywhere because it was loaded with precious family pictures. But she'd never found it and had finally given up, thinking she'd dropped it somewhere or it had fallen out of her car. But it wasn't lost! Apparently it had been in the Lincoln Aviator the whole time, perhaps lodged under a seat or wedged in a crack. When the car tumbled violently in the accident, the long-lost camera was dislodged and ended up loose in the car for Joe to find.

The camera still worked, and Nannette downloaded the photos. Among them were family pictures, including ones that included Ryan and Jane. There were photos of Ryan and Nannette together, a family Easter dinner get-together, and Nannette's last birthday celebration with her mother. Those precious memories had been locked away in the lost camera buried deep inside the car. The accident that took away something so precious also returned this small electronic device that bore cherished memories.

8

Leo's Bathroom Buddies

~~≈≈~~

The average dog is a nicer person
than the average person.

Andy Rooney

Leo was a massive dog. At 108 pounds he towered over most other pets. His huge head, wrinkly face, and powerful jaws frightened just about everyone on first glance. But Leo was a gentle giant. A bull-mastiff and Chinese shar-pei mix, he loved people and other animals—especially tiny ones.

Leo's special buddies were a little Chihuahua and a tiny kitten, each weighing in at less than 10 percent of Leo's body weight. In fact, the Chihuahua and the kitten were about the size of one of Leo's mighty paws.

The three unlikely pals lived together in a house in Kings County, California, an agricultural region in the Central Valley of the Golden State. Unfortunately the house had gone through foreclosure and the owners had fled the area without telling anyone. They left the three pets locked up together, without any food, in a bathroom inside the house. It was a horrible situation. Leo was tied with a cord to the toilet. The authorities estimated the two dogs and the kitten were stranded in the bathroom for two to three weeks. Thanks to neighbors who alerted the authorities, they survived.

"The three animals drank toilet water to survive and lasted weeks without food, with Leo never turning on his much smaller companions," wrote Monica Monzingo of Paw Nation, a Website dedicated to animal welfare. At some point the neighbors finally noticed the lack of activity at the house, heard some barking, and called the police. When authorities entered the home, they found a mess. Several dog crates were in the house with Chihuahuas inside. The animals had perished from lack of food and water.

The bathroom Leo and his pals were locked in was full of feces and urine from weeks of neglect. Leo and his bathroom buddies were starving and weak from their ordeal.

Unfortunately Leo's story is not unique. The mortgage crisis is causing some homeowners to leave their animals behind when they abandon their homes. "Pets are getting dumped all over," said Traci Jennings, president of a Humane Society in northern California. "Farmers are finding dogs dumped on their grazing grounds, while house cats are showing up in wild cat colonies."[1]

No one knows how many pets have been abandoned, but the situation has become widespread, according to anecdotal evidence from real estate agents and property inspectors. They've discovered dogs, cats, turtles, rabbits, birds, lizards, and horses left to fend for themselves. In Stockton, California, some homeowners trashed their home before the bank foreclosed, leaving a starving pit bull in the refuse. In Oklahoma, 24 horses were left on a ranch. Abandoned horses have been seen wandering the Florida everglades. In Glendale, California, three dogs left outside an abandoned foreclosed home without food or water for weeks were finally rescued by the local Humane Society. In that case, a good Samaritan had given food to the dogs to keep them alive until rescuers were able to legally remove them from the property.

A realty specialist estimated that one out of ten homeowners who goes through foreclosure leaves pets behind. The media has taken to calling these animals "Foreclosure Pets," and the ongoing problem has spawned a nonprofit organization called No Paws Left Behind, dedicated to rescuing pets abandoned due to foreclosure. "I've been in this business now for almost 20 years," said Robert Buchanan, a property inspector affiliated with No Paws Left Behind. "I come across this all the time. Sometimes you find them and the dogs are dead."[2]

One of animal welfare experts' greatest concerns, according to a *USA Today* article, is that pet owners who don't want their dogs and cats to be euthanized at a shelter set them loose instead. Or, like Leo, they are left in empty houses or garages. "Often the abandoned animals aren't found for days or weeks or are dead or dying,"[3] they say. The survivors ultimately wind up in a shelter anyway. Other pets set loose on the streets are infected with diseases, hit by cars, or injured in fights with other animals. While some foreclosure pets are euthanized, at least in a shelter they have a chance for adoption, don't endure the suffering of abandonment, and are given food and water.

Shelters are inundated with unwanted pets, and many of them have a hard time finding new homes for the stray animals. When Leo and his two buddies were rescued from their abandoned house in Kings County, they were taken to a local animal shelter where the three animals were nursed back to health. Leo was so emaciated that he had to put on some pounds before he could be given the needed vaccinations.

The shelter workers noticed a bond between the bullmastiff, the Chihuahua, and the kitten; Leo instantly cheered up whenever he saw the kitten. But after several months in the county shelter, the Chihuahua and the kitten were adopted by new families. Leo was not. The bullmastiff's large size and hefty appetite might have had something to do with the lack of interested families, especially in a county where the unemployment rates hovered around 15 percent. The county animal control facility was not a no-kill shelter, so Leo's time was running out.

That's when Tony La Russa's Animal Rescue Foundation (ARF) stepped in. ARF saves dogs and cats who have run out of time at public shelters, transports them to the private Adoption and Education

Center in the San Francisco Bay Area, and works to place them in stable, loving homes. "ARF strives to create a world where every loving dog and cat has a home," reads its mission statement.

Founder Tony La Russa is one of Major League Baseball's most recognized managers. His honors include Manager of the Year, along with his team's winning numerous titles, pennants, and World Series Championships. The catalyst for ARF came in May of 1990, during a baseball game between the Oakland Athletics, managed by La Russa, and the New York Yankees. A stray cat wandered onto the playing field. Terrified by the roar of the crowd, the cat ran for its life as umpires and players tried in vain to chase it down. Tony coaxed the cat into the dugout, securing its safety for the rest of the game. Afterward, he tried to place it with a local animal shelter but couldn't find a no-kill facility in the area. When he learned the cat was scheduled to be euthanized, he and his wife, Elaine, named the cat Evie and found her a home. Tony's time with Evie, and his experiences as a lifelong animal advocate, led to the founding of ARF. Thanks to Tony and Elaine's vision of no more homeless, unwanted pets, Leo had a chance for a new life.

The staff at ARF fell in love with Leo and decided to put the word out about the giant-but-lovable foreclosure dog. His story generated intense public interest, and Leo became a local celebrity. A cute picture of him with a Happy New Year crown on his big wrinkly head was seen all over the news. On January 2, the day Leo was eligible for adoption, several dozen people showed up to see him. Terry and Sandy O'Connor were second in line. They were shocked as the line of people behind them grew longer and longer. "We didn't realize what a rock star he was until we got there."

Fortunately, the O'Connors weren't strangers to large dogs. Their previous dog had been a bullmastiff that weighed in at 135 pounds. Bullmastiffs are descended from a cross between the English mastiff and the Old English bulldog. They were originally bred to be guard dogs and to find and immobilize poachers. The large breed is courageous, loyal, and become extremely attached to their families. They are confident but rarely aggressive.

The O'Connors' bullmastiff had been "a perfect house dog, extremely gentle and very docile. He'd been gone about five years, and we had no intention of getting another dog right away. We wanted to do some traveling and didn't want to take on the burden of a dog," said Terry. "But when we saw Leo's story we thought if we had the chance to give him a good home, we'd do that."

The people who were first in line took Leo into one of the get-acquainted rooms and then out for a walk. For some reason they decided not to take him. Then it was Terry and Sandy's turn. "The shelter lady warned me that Leo was kind of fearful of men and didn't like baseball caps. When we met him he kind of ignored me, walked right up to my wife, sat down, and stared right into her eyes," said Terry. "She was crying in about two seconds. He just stared at her. She was sold."

Sandy had been the one who had wanted to hold off on getting a dog because "we want to do some traveling." But Leo "melted her. She just looked into his eyes and could tell what he'd been through."

And the part about Leo not liking men? "I called him over to me, and he was fine. He seemed very friendly and very docile for such a big dog." They decided to adopt him. And it was a good thing they decided quickly because the people next in line wanted to take him home too.

In the end it was almost like Leo picked the O'Connors. "We believe it was meant to be." Leo has turned out to be a very gentle dog who gets along with just about everyone and everything, including the family's two cats. They were pretty sure he would, based on his bond with his bathroom buddy kitten. And that turned out to be a good indicator. "Leo couldn't wait to make friends with our cat, and our male cat is just in love with Leo," said Terry. "They are best buddies. They hang out together during the day and sleep together too." The O'Connors' son has an energetic Chihuahua-pit bull mix that comes over to play. "It becomes a wrestling match. They play for hours."

So although Leo didn't get to stay with his two bathroom buddies, he's made lots of friends in his new home. After all that Leo has gone through, it's a miracle that he still trusts people. "Leo's got it made," said Terry. "I don't think he looks back at all. That's in the past, and he's living right now, in the moment. He's just as happy as can be."

Leo's favorite spot is a big pillow in front of the fireplace. Terry and Sandy take him on a walk every night, and when they put on their tennis shoes, Leo knows it's time to go. He loves to play. "He doesn't have an aggressive bone in his body," said Terry. And when it's time for bed, he stretches out on his own memory foam mattress.

"He deserves a good life here," said Terry.

If there's a lesson to be learned from Leo's ordeal, according to Terry, it's that people who want pets should look for rescue animals first. "Give these animals a chance" rather than buying from a breeder. "A lot of them are on death row or close to it. If ARF had not gotten involved, Leo's time would have been up. That's the thing we don't understand. He's a perfect dog. He's not aggressive by any means. We can't see why somebody didn't take him before ARF found him," Terry said.

A few years ago, a woman in Georgia adopted a stray bullmastiff and took the dog she named Honey fishing on a pier off the Chattahoochee Riverwalk.[4] Later that evening a man attacked her, hit her on the head, and knocked her out. She came to while the man was trying to sexually assault her. Although Honey was tied to a nearby rail, the dog chewed through her leash, grabbed the attacker's shirt, pulled him off the woman, and chased him down the pier. I'm guessing the man will think twice before he tries something like that again.

9

Making the Rounds with Blackie

When confronted with the healing presence of an animal,
I am warmed by a sense of hope for the world.

CASEY CARPENTER

When Blackie walks through the doorway of a hospice center to visit sick children, he generates a ripple of excitement. The kids love to pet him and groom his silky black fur. He is gentle and quiet, but his eyes are alive and seem to be saying, "Let's do this!" His ears point forward and he exudes life and energy. A wise man once said that gentleness is "strength under control." That's Blackie.

Therapy dogs are now a common sight in health-care facilities. They bring hope and happiness to people who are ill. And Blackie is a natural, achieving the highest level of certification from Pet Partners, a program from the Delta Society that trains volunteers and their pets for animal visiting programs in hospitals, nursing homes, rehabilitation centers, schools, and other facilities.

Most therapy animals are dogs who have been partnering with

humans for thousands of years to serve in a variety of roles. They are quick to establish a strong, therapeutic human–animal bond.

But Blackie is *not* a dog. He's a horse. A miniature horse with a very big job. While most children have either owned a dog or been around dogs, many kids don't get opportunities to be around horses. So it's a very special moment when Blackie clip-clops down the hallway, stops at a sick child's door, pokes his head in, and then enters. Blackie's visits must seem too good to be true for a family that has often heard too much bad news.

"Blackie is our superstar," shared Melanie Buerke of SonRise Equestrian Foundation, a nonprofit organization that creates loving connections between horses and people (especially children) living with social, emotional, or physical challenges. SonRise puts children on specially trained horses with close supervision for individualized programs of instruction. By learning how to handle and ride horses, children develop confidence, integrity, and a sense of responsibility, along with working on physical, emotional, and cognitive skills. SonRise has full-size and miniature horses. Blackie is one of six "minis" and very special.

"Blackie knows what to do and how to approach the kids. [He] has a thoughtfulness. His eyes are just expressive, present, *there*. You can look at Blackie and ask him for something. He'll think about it, and then usually do it," said Melanie.

Good therapy animals need to like people, be controllable and teachable, have good manners, and a stable personality. They also have to calmly accept new or unusual sights, sounds, smells, and situations. Blackie fulfills every requirement, plus he passionately loves children.

Melanie never planned on working with miniatures. Right after SonRise got started, Melanie and some of her volunteers were sitting around brainstorming, daydreaming out loud how to get the word out about the services they offer the community. "Wouldn't it be great if we had a miniature horse?" someone announced. "We could take it around to festivals and parades. Can you imagine how much attention it would get?" Everyone agreed, but they had no idea where to go or how to find one.

Then Melanie received an unusual phone call. "I heard about who you guys are and what you're doing," a woman said. "I have a little miniature horse named Blackie. He's been a show horse, performed in parades, pulls a cart, and has lots of training. And he *loves* kids. I'm getting married and moving to Switzerland, and I'm pretty sure I won't be able to take him with me. I want to meet you and see if your organization is a good place for Blackie to go."

The woman came out to the ranch, which is located in the grassy, golden foothills across the bay from San Francisco. Melanie showed her around the immaculate barns and introduced her to the foundation's gentle, well-mannered, and intelligent horses. She met with some of the volunteers and heard more about the vision—to help hurting children thrive by receiving unconditional love from a concerned mentor and a special horse at no cost to their caregivers. The woman left knowing her highly trained and loving little horse would have a very special job at SonRise.

So Blackie moved in and everyone fell in love with him. None of the SonRise women had ever worked with a mini before, but they soon discovered that Blackie has the same characteristics as a full-sized horse—just offered in a smaller package. Blackie is about the size of a large Rottweiler or German shepherd. He has a shiny black coat and a fluffy black mane and tail. He's surprisingly strong and can pull a cart with two people in it. He can also be ridden by small children who might be afraid of riding and handling a larger horse.

Sometimes people confuse miniature horses with ponies, another type of small horse. The most familiar ponies are Shetlands, measuring around 42 inches. They have sturdy bodies with short legs and a bushy mane and tail. Ponies are often stubborn and difficult to train. They are descended from "pit ponies" that were used to haul loads of coal up from the mines during the Industrial Revolution in Great Britain.

Miniature horses were used as pit ponies too, but more commonly minis were bred as pets for European nobility. In the 1600s, King Louis XIV of France kept miniature horses in his zoo. The small horses became a hot commodity in the 1700s and were depicted in news articles and paintings of the period. Over the last two centuries, minis have been used as pets, as well as for research, monetary gain, exhibition, and royal gifts. Minis started becoming popular in the United States in the 1960s.

Minis are hardy and often live longer than larger breeds. One advantage of using horses as therapy animals is that they live much longer than dogs. The oldest living horse on record was Angel, a dwarf mini who lived to the age of 50. Most minis live between 25 to 35 years. The smallest horse on record is Thumbelina, a dwarf mini who stands 17 inches tall, weighs 60 pounds, and lives at Goose Creek Farms in St. Louis, Missouri.

In the last few years minis have been used as guides for the blind and for helping to pull wheelchairs. While the practice is controversial, there are some advantages. Minis have acute vision. With eyes located on the sides of their heads, they enjoy a nearly 350-degree visual field. Horses are sensitive to motion and often detect hazards before their sighted trainers. Minis don't get fleas. And with their longer life spans, they might prove to be a good return on the costly investment in terms of time and money for the training of service animals.

As Melanie got to know Blackie and watched him in action at community events, she was impressed with his calm, soothing personality. He wasn't lazy or passive, and his active mind was obvious by the way he watched whatever was going on, ears up and forward. He had plenty of get-up-and-go and was always quick to learn and to perform, but his energy was carefully harnessed for whatever the situation required.

Then Melanie got another unexpected call. One of the SonRise volunteers worked at a local respite care and end-of-life facility for children. She wondered if Melanie would bring Blackie over to visit the sick children at the hospice? Melanie wasn't sure how Blackie would react to being indoors, especially in a medical facility. *Would the unfamiliar environment bother him? Would he be able to tolerate the beeps and buzzes of the various monitors and the smells of disinfectants and medications?*

There was only one way to find out. Melanie collected a couple of volunteers to help and loaded Blackie in the horse trailer for the short ride to the hospice. When they arrived, he surprised everyone by walking right in like he owned the place. Melanie started with short visits to the facility, gradually acquainting Blackie with his new job. She watched for signs of nervousness or stress and always took him home before he might become uncomfortable.

Melanie decided to take Blackie through the certification process for Pet Partners at Delta. "It was incredible," said Melanie. "We went through training together, and Blackie was dynamite. During the test to see how Blackie might react in unusual situations, they tried to scare him with loud noises, a guy hit him on the hindquarters and yelled, and they shook noisemakers around him. There was some weird stuff going on! But Blackie just stood and looked."

The tiny horse graduated from the program with flying colors and was certified at the highest level. He and Melanie began to visit the children at the hospice regularly. It wasn't long before Blackie felt right at home. Every month, Blackie and Melanie made the rounds, the mini marching into each room and allowing himself to be stroked and brushed and patted, spreading his own fuzzy brand of hope and healing.

"It's almost like magic," Melanie said. "We go into a room where a child is ill. The mom, dad, and siblings will be there, all sitting around the edges of the bed and so sad. Sometimes I feel like I could cut the atmosphere with a knife because it's so heavy with grief and pain. But Blackie walks in, clip-clop, and everything changes. It's like he brings light and fresh air into the room. It's a moment no one ever forgets."

Blackie also visits convalescent homes where the elderly people love him too. His presence often reminds them of happy childhood memories of horses. For many of them, horses were part of daily life while growing up. Petting Blackie helps them remember those happy times. He is just as comfortable with an older person as he is with a child.

After Blackie had been making his rounds for a few months, a call came in with an emergency request for a special, unscheduled visit. A little girl named Francine was very ill. Her parents had checked her into the end-of-life facility so she could spend the last part of her life in a comfortable, cheerful place where her family could enjoy time together in a life-affirming, supportive environment.

Francine loved horses, and when Melanie walked into the room she noticed a fluffy stuffed horse on the dresser. The room was awash in sadness. The parents were huddled in one corner, and Francine's grandmother was in the other corner. In the middle of the room was the bed where Francine lay. She had been in and out of a comatose state for a while now, and it was almost impossible to rouse her.

Then in walked Blackie, clip-clop, ears perky and eyes shining, life and love and energy in a compact package of fur and tail and hooves. He looked around, took in the room, and then approached the bed. He walked up until his chest gently bumped against the covers, and he gently lowered his head onto the bed. His chin and whiskery lips ever so softly nudged the girl's hand.

The nurse gently shook Francine's arm. "Honey, Blackie's here." No response. The little girl slept on.

"Francine, Blackie's here to see you," the nurse repeated.

Francine stirred, moved her head, and slowly opened her eyes. Her parents, who had been waiting in the corner to see what would happen, jumped up. Francine was waking up.

Melanie talked softly to the girl, and when she seemed ready, helped her reach over and touch Blackie's head. His fur radiated warmth and life, and the girl stroked him, her hand moving slowly. Her eyes opened wider and her body shifted a bit. Then she smiled as she looked at Blackie, and the room suddenly grew brighter.

Melanie understands exactly what a horse means to a little girl. She grew up in a very dysfunctional home and was 11 years old when her father left. Her mother couldn't cope and disappeared from home for days, sometimes weeks. Melanie had very little supervision or stability. She grew up loving horses, as many girls do. "Right before my mom checked out, she bought me a horse. Through the grace of God and with the help of that horse, I made it through my teenage years," Melanie says. As a young adult, she didn't have much time for horses. When her mother came down with cancer, Melanie had nowhere else to turn for comfort. She decided to get another horse and fell in love with a beautiful white mare named Celeste.

Celeste had been a national show horse trained in Saddle Seat Show Ride, a dramatic style of performance that's big, fast, and theatrical. Horses trained in this style are very hard for the average person to ride, and Melanie needed some instruction. One of the first times she tried to approach Celeste, the horse reared up in her stall and frightened her. "But there was something about that horse that resonated," said Melanie. With her mother dying of cancer, Melanie needed something to hold on to. "Celeste kept me together," said Melanie. "She gave me a reason to get out of bed every day."

The beautiful white horse seemed to sense Melanie's feelings. After her mom died, Melanie went into Celeste's stall every day and cried into the horse's mane. "That horse brought incredible healing, and that time with her was the impetus for SonRise. I wanted a place where hurting, broken children can find healing. If it weren't for Celeste, I wouldn't be here."

There is something majestic and beautiful and powerful when a horse trusts someone enough to make friends. Like dogs, horses live in community, and when they allow a human into that community, there is a special bond.

Everyone in Francine's room felt that bond grow between the girl and Blackie. Francine's smile grew, and her parents took pictures as she sat up, propped by pillows, and slowly brushed Blackie with a soft bristle brush Melanie put in her hand. Blackie kept his head quiet, allowing the girl to groom his mane and forelock. For about 15 minutes, Francine was happy, lighting up the room with her shining face as she talked to the little black horse whose head was perched on her bed. Then Francine grew tired, lay back, and began to fade. As the child's eyes grew heavy and she got drowsy Melanie knew it was time to leave. She took Blackie's lead rope and led him quietly out of the room, glancing one last time at Francine and then at her stuffed horse. This was the wonderful day when Francine made friends with a real horse.

The next day Melanie heard what happened after she and Blackie left. Francine was tired but awake and alert enough to talk to her mom, dad, and grandma. She told them how much she loved them, and they spent some precious moments together. It was a bittersweet time because Francine's body was failing. But the visit from Blackie had woken the little girl up, put a smile on her face, and unlocked an outpouring of love and tenderness between the family members, allowing them the chance to say goodbye. That was the last time Francine was awake. But some of her last moments were spent with Blackie, her hand on his soft nose, his warm breath tickling her skin.

The story of Blackie is not a dog tale…and this is a book about dogs. But since Blackie is doing a therapy-animal job most people associate with dogs, I thought I would sneak it in. One of the most amazing horse tales to come out of SonRise is about Jenny, an autistic girl who was afraid of horses. When she visited a ranch, she kept repeating "No horse" anytime she got close to one. She did show interest in a metal horse figure and climbed onto it, pretending to ride. She later visited SonRise Equestrian for a "Horse Play Day," but again she said, "No horse." She watched other kids riding, but kept repeating her no horse mantra.

Then her mother said, "Okay, Jenny's turn." Jenny surprised everyone by jumping onto the horse's back and taking a turn around the arena with her parents walking alongside. The first real lesson started with a loud crying session, but by the end Jenny was hugging and nuzzling her horse. In the next few weeks instead of "No horse," Jenny said, "More horse." Jenny has now learned to ride. She knows the parts of a horse and has participated in grooming, saddling, and riding. She can walk, trot, and canter on her horse, as well as play games like Around the World, spinning herself around on the saddle. She is learning to follow directions, showing natural athletic ability, and forming a strong bond with her four-legged friend. The little girl who used to be afraid of animals now loves horses, along with the dogs and cats who live on the ranch. Jenny's smile is bright, but what really shines are the smiles of her mom and dad as they watch their daughter, once locked in her solitary world, blossom on the back of a horse.

10

Papa Loves You, Kaiser

~~✖~~

Promise me you'll never forget me because if
I thought you would, I'd never leave.

Winnie the Pooh (A.A. Milne)

It was a routine morning for Debbie Herot, manager of a full-service veterinary hospital in the San Fernando Valley, just north of Los Angeles. After zipping down the Pacific Coast Highway, she arrived at work. Her early morning commute was an hour-and-a-half long, and she usually arrived while it was still dark.

The veterinary hospital was open 24 hours a day. There were two entrances—one opening into a cat reception area and one opening into a dog reception area. This time Debbie entered through the cat reception area. On her way in the front door she had to step over a big black dog lying on a blanket. *That's odd*, she thought. *Where's the owner?*

She found a tech in the back room. "Whose dog is that in front of the door?" Debbie asked.

In response, the tech handed Debbie a letter. "Here, I couldn't get halfway through without crying. Just read it," the tech urged.

Debbie took a deep breath and unfolded the letter. It was a half sheet of white paper covered in neat pencil writing. She noticed the beautiful penmanship. On the envelope, a neat pencil note said the dog, named Kaiser, had experienced two strokes the night before.

She took another breath and began to read.

Dear Doctors,

Please forgive me for this horrible transgression. I have nowhere else to turn so I ask you to mercifully, gently, and lovingly please help him sleep. His name is Kaiser, and he's 16-and-a-half years old. He's been my friend, my teacher, my pupil, my lifelong loving and loyal companion. He's gentle, smart, and I'll miss him more than I could admit. Be good to him as you would your own child for he's been mine for a loving lifetime. We've been together 24/7, 365 days a year since he was eight months old.

Saturday evening, without warning or any outside influence, he began rolling on his back on the floor, all four legs extended, rigid, and thrusting wildly in all directions. I saw fear and panic in his otherwise unrecognizable eyes. He can stand, but he is 85 percent unsteady. He's fearfully reacting to attempts to get him to drink water. He refuses food as though he's totally lost the knowledge of what to do with it. I'm a homeless, disabled veteran, and I know when to say goodbye to a friend—and his time is now. He's such a part of my being, I'll once again be alone in my life.

Please tell Kaiser I love him. Thank you for caring.

Sincerely,
Kaiser's Soul Mate

There was no name or other identifying information anywhere on the letter.

"How's the dog?" Debbie asked the tech.

"He's still alive," the tech said.

Debbie's eyes filled with tears. As manager of the hospital she ran the business, and she tried to maintain a comfortable emotional distance from the animals. The dog she had stepped over looked ill. He was old. Usually an abandoned animal in such poor shape would be quickly euthanized. But this time, she couldn't give the order without having him checked out. *This dog is not going to doggie heaven yet.*

Debbie asked the tech for more details. Kaiser had been discovered with a blanket, a bowl of water, an extra water bottle, and the envelope containing the letter. Around the envelope had been wrapped a black cord with a hand-carved wooden cross, about three inches high, dangling from it. On the back of the cross was inscribed "Papa Loves You Kaiser."

When they went back out to get the dog, Kaiser was standing quietly, although he hadn't moved from the blanket.

Debbie was determined to help this dog, so beloved by the letter writer. She rallied the rest of the clinic employees to Kaiser's cause and the work began. "I was pretty emotional at first, but once I got the staff involved, it became more of a mission. Kaiser was pretty close to death when we found him," said Debbie. "Our doctors worked hard. Money wasn't an issue. We knew Kaiser was special."

Financial aid for Kaiser's veterinary care came from someone near and dear to the clinic employees. Just the year before, a 23-year-old employee named Eric Flesher had died in a car crash. His family had started a special fund to help pay for veterinary care for animals like Kaiser because Eric "used to hate seeing animals come in that couldn't get treatment because their owners couldn't afford the cost of the care,"[1] Debbie shared. Eric's fund was used to care for Kaiser. "We weren't sure if we could save him, but we were going to give it a try."

One of the veterinarians determined that Kaiser had not had a serious stroke after all. Instead, it may have been a mild stroke that caused vestibular disease, similar to vertigo in humans. There was a good chance for recovery. On the fourth day after his arrival, Kaiser began to drink water on his own. On the fifth day, he was eating, walking, and even running. Over the course of a week, Kaiser slowly recuperated from his ordeal, and Debbie saw his personality emerge. "He was a love—really a love," she said. "He was a Dobie mix, and he was smart."

Doberman pinschers are well known as intelligent, alert, and loyal companions often used as guard dogs and police dogs. Although Dobermans are sometimes unfairly characterized as aggressive, they are extremely loyal and trainable. Several dog intelligence studies have consistently shown that Dobermans, border collies, German shepherds, and standard poodles are the most trainable breeds of dog. At more than 16 years of age, Kaiser was pretty old for a Doberman mix. Most Dobermans live 10 to 14 years and suffer from a wide range of health issues. Kaiser's advanced age and his survival from this recent health episode were a testament to the loving and meticulous care he'd received from his anonymous owner.

Now that Kaiser was recovering, it was time to try to find his master. Whoever had dropped him off and written the letter probably thought Kaiser was long gone, dispatched by a compassionate veterinarian through euthanasia. But Kaiser's owner was due for some very good news if Debbie and her crew could get the word out around the community so he would hear it.

Debbie guessed the owner lived in the area. Because he loved his dog so much, no doubt he had scoped out the clinic to make sure it was the best place to leave his old friend.

The clinic employees spread the word and hung hundreds of posters. A newspaper columnist for Los Angeles' *Daily News* ran a story on Kaiser and the hunt for his homeless owner. The front-page story ran with the headline: "Dear Veteran: Your best pal's waiting to go home."

Debbie was excited that the media was getting involved in the search, but she was also worried that because of the public attention, someone other than the owner might show up and try to take Kaiser home. No one had seen Kaiser's owner, so how would they know it was really him? Plus Kaiser was so friendly and loving, he might be willing to go with anyone. Then Debbie hit on a plan. If someone showed up claiming to be the owner, she would meet with him alone. Then she would pose a key question: *What object had been left with the letter?* If the man was Kaiser's true owner, he would be able to describe the cross, which hadn't been mentioned on the posters or in the news story.

One day Los Angeles TV Station KTLA sent a crew out to the clinic to film a story on the search for Kaiser's owner. By a strange coincidence, while the television crew was there a man named Bob Mikolasko showed up. He walked in and told the receptionist he was there to pick up Kaiser. The reception staff, excited, paged Debbie. She directed them to take Bob to an examination room. Kaiser was on leash with a tech nearby but out of sight.

Debbie joined Bob in the room and chatted with him a bit. She filled him in on Kaiser's condition. She could tell the man was nervous and excited. She asked, heart pounding, "Can you tell me what was wrapped around the envelope that you left with Kaiser that morning?"

"Yes. A brown wooden cross with 'Papa Loves You, Kaiser' engraved on it," Bob replied.

"Bingo!" said Debbie with a big smile. "Follow me. Kaiser's waiting outside for you."

No one could have known Bob was coming in that particular day, but the KTLA television crew was still onsite and they filmed Bob and Kaiser's reunion. When Bob saw his dog, he dropped to his knees. Kaiser mobbed him, joyfully wagging his tail and licking Bob's face. The dog's elderly body wiggled happily as he nudged up against Bob. "His tail almost knocked over the cameras," Debbie said with a laugh.

Debbie found out that Bob was 56 years old and a disabled vet. He and Kaiser had lived in a motor home parked on the streets for 14 years and in the garage of a friend for the past two years. When Kaiser had started acting ill, Bob was sure he was dying but didn't have enough money to pay for him to be euthanized. So he had written the letter, bundled up the dog and his water bowl, and left him at the clinic doorstep. The wooden cross had been Kaiser's homemade dog tag. Bob never expected to see Kaiser alive again.

The pain Bob experienced at losing his best friend must have been intense. While people experience grief in different ways, pet owners often feel guilt for an accident or illness that takes their pets' lives, even if they are not responsible. Sometimes there is denial, making it difficult to accept the loss of a pet. Anger is also a common reaction, directed at the illness or at themselves. And, of course, many experience depression, a natural reaction to grief that takes away motivation, energy, and the ability to cope with feelings. Intense grief over the loss of a pet is normal and natural.[2]

When it comes time to euthanize a beloved pet, some people want to be present to love and comfort the animal. But for many, being present is heart-wrenching and too painful to witness. Bob made the best decision he could. He didn't want to prolong his dog's suffering, but he couldn't bear to watch either. So he put Kaiser in good hands, trusting the clinic to take care of his friend. And the clinic, spearheaded by Debbie's passion to reunite a healthy dog with his much-loved owner, didn't let him down.

A week after he dropped Kaiser off at the clinic, someone showed him the news story on the front page of the newspaper. Bob rushed down to the clinic, excited that his best friend was still alive. After a tearful and joyous reunion, Bob drove off in his old truck. Kaiser had his head hanging out the window and his tail was wagging double time. "There wasn't a dry eye in the house," Debbie said, including her own.

The experience changed Debbie's life. "Had anybody else walked in first that morning or if I had been out sick, the dog probably would have been euthanized," she said. "It broke my heart to think about what Bob went through that morning when he dropped the dog off. Even the torture of writing that letter..."

"But look what we could do," she said. "It was meant to be."

A couple of days later, Bob showed up at the clinic again. Kaiser looked happy and sported a yellow bandanna around his neck. Bob thanked Debbie and her crew. Debbie gave Bob the blanket, freshly laundered, that he'd used to wrap Kaiser in when he left him on the clinic's doorstep.

Bob gave Debbie the small wooden cross that had been wrapped around the envelope. She treasures it, along with the letter. But Bob had given Debbie much more than a wooden cross. He also gave her new eyes. "I learned not to always look the other way," she admitted. "And I've learned to be more compassionate in every area of my life."

A few months after Bob and Kaiser were reunited, Kaiser finally did pass away. He had cancer, and his body was just too old to fight it. But the two best friends made the most of their remaining time together, and Bob enjoyed every minute. "He's got a heart of gold," said Debbie. She and Bob have become fast friends. Strangely, after Kaiser died, Bob also came down with cancer. He went to a VA hospital every day for a while to undergo chemotherapy. He lost weight and became very weak, but after treatment ended, he rallied. Debbie saw him recently and said he looks fantastic. He still drops in once in a while for a visit. He currently lives in his truck in a friend's driveway. He doesn't have a new dog yet. It may take him a while to find a dog like Kaiser. When he's ready, Debbie will be there to help.

11

Polishing the Black Pearl

~≈~

Properly trained, a man can be a dog's best friend.

COREY FORD

Pearl was a fence jumper. Not the kind of fence jumper that has special agility training and jumps cute little white fences on command, but the kind of dog that refuses to stay in a yard because there is a big, wide world out there and a wimpy five-foot fence is not going to stop her. So Pearl jumped the fence every day and went out to explore.

A Labrador retriever with a gleaming black coat, Pearl had a big heart, loved people, and was always looking for fun. She belonged to a young man who put her out in the backyard each day when he went to work. As soon as he left, she jumped the fence and headed out to roam the streets of the small northern California town where they lived.

Pearl was a regular visitor—or perhaps inmate would be a better word—at the local animal shelter. Someone would see her roaming around and call animal control. The officers would pick her up and check her into the shelter. The shelter would call Pearl's owner to come in. He'd trek in, pay the fine to bail out his dog, and take her home. And the next day she would do it again. It didn't take long for the owner to run out of money to pay the fines. And he couldn't figure out how to keep Pearl in his yard. He liked her, but he couldn't cope with the demands of such an intelligent and high-energy dog. He surrendered her to the shelter, and Pearl's days of running loose on the streets were over.

Pearl languished at the animal shelter for a month. While she was friendly, her extreme energy intimidated people. And being locked up in a small enclosure for an extended period didn't help matters.

A local rescue group called High Sierra Animal Rescue has volunteers that regularly tour the county animal shelter in search of adoptable dogs. Pearl's friendly face, wagging tale, and shiny, energetic body caught one volunteer's eye, and he decided to take her. His car was already full of dogs, but he knew he could make room for one more. He signed her out of the shelter.

Back at High Sierra Animal Rescue, they dubbed the Labrador "The Black Pearl" for her beautiful coat. They couldn't help but notice her high energy and intelligence and thought that what Pearl needed was not a fence she couldn't jump over but a new line of work that would take advantage of her very special personality. It was time to get Bark Force involved.

Bark Force is the recruiting arm of the Search Dog Foundation, which trains Disaster Search Dogs to find people buried alive in the aftermath of earthquakes, mudslides, and building collapses. These dogs undergo specialized training for a year. They are taught to recognize a specific smell—the scent of a living person. The dogs can climb over and explore a large pile of rubble very quickly, which is crucial when someone is buried alive and every second counts.

The best breeds for Search and Rescue are working dogs such as golden retrievers, border collies, German shepherds, and Labrador retrievers. Bark Force also looks for high energy, athletic dogs who love to play fetch and are good at finding lost toys. The Search Dog Foundation has rescued hundreds of dogs, many on the brink of euthanasia, trained them, and then partnered them with firefighters. The dogs and training are provided at no cost to community fire departments because the funding comes from individuals, companies, and private foundations. So far they have trained 105 search teams that respond to disasters in the United States and across the world.

Pearl fit every requirement, and her hyperactive personality made her a perfect candidate. Bark Force member Penny Woodruff visited High Sierra to evaluate Pearl, using the "toy drive test," designed to test for an unusually high "prey drive"—the determination a dog shows to find a hidden toy. When Pearl passed that evaluation, she was sent to Portola for a second evaluation. "Within the first five minutes of the testing process, I knew we had a winner," said Karen Klingberg, Search Dog Foundation's canine manager. It's not a slam-dunk test. Typically only 1 out of 100 dogs successfully pass and are accepted into the program.

Pearl was a natural. Karen noticed immediately she could barely sit still. All the dog could think about was finding and retrieving the toy used in the test. She found it again and again, even when it went into some thorny shrubs. "She would disappear over the dune and into the thicket. I couldn't even see her. A few minutes later she would pop out with the toy in her mouth, ready to do it again." Pearl's explosive energy never flagged.

The once unwanted dog was about to leave her fence jumping past far behind. Instead, her energy would now be harnessed to save lives. Karen loaded her up into her van and drove downstate so Pearl could begin formal Search Dog Training.

Search Dog Training is an intense six- to eight-month period of search-and-rescue training, much like military boot camp. When Pearl finished this part of her training, she was assigned to Ron Horetski, a captain with the Los Angeles County Fire Department. Ron has been a firefighter for 21 years. He loves helping people and worked in New Orleans after Hurricane Katrina. He's been doing search-and-rescue work and training for 8 years.

When he heard about Pearl's availability, Ron was excited. He's always loved dogs and had been a handler with the Search Dog Foundation for over a year with his German shepherd named Fritzie. "We tried to get Fritzie certified for two years," said Ron. "But she was too slow on the rubble pile test—where a 10,000-square-foot rubble pile has to be completely searched in just 20 minutes." The rubble pile test is difficult to pass because testers try to distract the dogs from finding the "victims," people posing as victims of a collapse. Distractions include food, live chickens, and even cats. The dogs fail if they get off task.

After Fritzie was released from duty as a search dog, Ron needed a new partner. Pearl and Ron were paired up and began training together. When Pearl was given the rubble pile test, she completed a search of the debris in just over 12 minutes. She found 3 "victims." Because of the sensitivity of the canine nose, search dogs can smell people trapped 3 to 10 feet underground and are trained to bark when they find someone alive. "It all depends on the 'hyperness' of the dog," Ron explained. "The more hyper the dog, the better." Pearl's abundance of energy was finally paying off for her. "Pearl is like a bullet over any terrain," Ron said.

Before long, Ron and Pearl earned certification with the Federal Emergency Management Agency (FEMA). The dog who was once a lost cause was now part of an elite team of search dogs trained to rescue people. Shortly after certification, Ron and Pearl were deployed to a building collapse in La Puente, California. Ten people were reported missing. When they arrived, Ron saw that the façade on the front of the mall had collapsed. Ron and Pearl were ordered to search the outside and inside of the building. They did and came up with nothing. Everyone had made it safely out of the building. Pearl did her job perfectly. Her reward? A quick game of tug-of-war or fetch with a dog toy. It's what Pearl loves best.

Ron and Pearl settled into a routine. Part of serving on Los Angeles County Task Force 2 is maintaining readiness for deployment anywhere in the United States or the world as one of the two FEMA Task Forces able to deploy internationally. Ron and Pearl are together almost 24/7.

They rise early and leave each morning at four o'clock, with Pearl riding in her kennel in the back of Ron's truck. When they arrive at the fire station, Pearl takes her place in a special kennel. Ron has trained the other fire fighters at the station to take care of his valuable dog if she were to get injured or become ill when he's not there, but otherwise he is the only one who handles her at work.

On the afternoon of January 12, 2010, the Haiti earthquake struck. Measuring 7.0 on the Richter Scale, the earthquake was disastrous, causing heavy building damage and loss of life. Buildings crumpled all over the island and many people, dead and alive, were trapped in the rubble. The earthquake leveled the capital city of Port-au-Prince that had a population of two million people. Within hours of the earthquake, Ron and Pearl got the call. They would be flying to Haiti to do search and rescue.

Ron, Pearl, and the rest of the Search and Rescue team flew to Haiti aboard a C-17 Globemaster, a military cargo plane, out of March Air Force Base in Riverside, California. They arrived in Port-Au-Prince at six o'clock in the morning on January 14 and immediately went to work. The team brought 48 tons of special equipment, tools, food, and water.

The task force's canine team has six search-and-rescue dogs and their handlers, divided into a red team and a blue team. Ron was on the red team, assigned to start searching at a collapsed hotel. Later Ron's team was assigned to an eight-block area of the city, and after that, an outlying suburb. Conditions were dangerous, and Ron and Pearl drew on their training to stay safe and to search effectively. When they had time to rest, the task force lived in tents on the grounds of the United States Embassy, guarded by troops from the United Nations.

The dogs and handlers found a number of people alive in the wreckage. CNN filmed one of the most dramatic saves: a woman was rescued from a collapsed three-story office building. Somehow she had survived in a 14-inch void in the wreckage.

Three young girls trapped in the rubble of a four-story building were discovered alive by a border collie search dog named Hunter. The girls had been trapped for nearly 70 hours. The dog's handler was able to speak to the girls and then pass them bottles of water tied to the end of a stick.[1] One of the little girls said "Thank you" in English.

Another rescue involved the discovery of a 50-year-old woman inside a collapsed building. She was pulled to safety and suffered from slight injuries and dehydration.

Whenever searchers find people alive, the team works to get water to them before anything else. If possible, a paramedic crawls through the debris to get close enough to the survivors to start IVs. If that isn't possible, the team works hard to get water to them any way possible. Ron said in one case the team was able to set up a PVC pipe that dripped water into a survivor's mouth. After giving the survivors vital fluids, the effort to remove them begins.

After 14 days in Haiti, searching countless piles of rubble and pulling out people alive and dead, Ron and Pearl and the rest of the Search and Rescue teams were sent home when the Haitian government ended the operation. Altogether the teams rescued 45 people. The California Task Force, including Pearl, rescued 12 of them.

The Haiti mission was the first international mission for the California Task Force. In the beginning the Haitian people were suspicious of the team. Some locals thought a bomb had exploded; others thought the Americans were engaged in a military effort. But the firefighters explained their mission and invited the Haitians to work with them. After one woman was pulled from the wreckage of a hotel, the crowd in the street began chanting "USA! USA! USA!"

When Ron, Pearl, and the rest of the task force returned from Haiti, they received a hero's welcome from friends and family. Ron told one reporter that "in spite of the death and destruction, looting and lawlessness, heat and humidity, he would go back in a heartbeat."[2]

All of the hours of hard work, training, and practice paid dividends in human lives. And the dogs who had once been rescued were now returning the favor by helping rescue people in a timely manner. Thanks to the Bark Force, who found Pearl in the animal shelter, she's moved on from jumping fences and roaming the streets to jumping into rubble and saving lives! Pearl's energy has been harnessed for a higher purpose, and like a highly polished gemstone, this pearl shines.

I first discovered Pearl and Ron's story through an article in the paper about a children's book self-published by a second-grade class in Alamo, California. The book is called *A New Job for Pearl: A Homeless Dog Becomes a Hero,* and is the third in a series created by veteran teacher Connie Forslind and volunteer Allyn Lee at Rancho Romero Elementary School. Allyn wrote the text, and the children drew the illustrations. The full-color book had a printing of 3000 copies, and all the proceeds from the book sales go to the National Disaster Search Dog Foundation. The children's goal is to raise $10,000 for the training of one search-and-rescue dog like Pearl. For more information, go to www.anewjobforpearl.org.

The book starts out: "This is the true story of a once-homeless dog that became part of a Search and Rescue team. Pearl is a black Labrador retriever with bright eyes, a smiling face, and a tail that will not stay still." When the book was finished, Ron and Pearl flew up from Los Angeles to visit the class. The kids loved Pearl, and Pearl loved the kids. Everyone noticed her "crazy energy," said Allyn. "Exactly the reason these dogs don't make good pets and are often abandoned. But her energy was harnessed by her intense focus on Ron. It is clear that she adores him!"

12

Running with Roselle

~≈~

Histories are more full of examples of the
fidelity of dogs than of friends.

ALEXANDER POPE

Roselle likes to lie in the sun. She's a senior citizen now and has arthritis in her hips. This restricts the movement in her back legs, causing them to twist slightly inward, so walking is an effort. She also has an autoimmune disorder, so she has regular blood work to monitor her condition. She sleeps a lot, stretched out in the sunlight streaming through the sliding glass door, her two best friends bookending her at head and at tail. They are yellow Labrador retrievers just like Roselle.

But Roselle has seen and heard and lived through things her friends Fantasia and Africa never will. It's not obvious by looking at her dozing in the sun, but Roselle is a Congressionally recognized national hero. Along with her owner Michael Hingson, Roselle survived the World Trade Center attacks on September 11, 2001.

Michael is blind and Roselle was his guide dog.

The day started in the dark for Michael and Roselle in their New Jersey house. Roselle woke Michael at 12:30 in the morning, nosing his hand and quivering in fear as a thunderstorm approached. "She can tell when a storm is brewing," Michael shared. "She usually gets nervous about 30 minutes before the thunder rolls in."

Michael tried to soothe her, stroking her head and talking in a soft voice. But she wouldn't be comforted. In panic, she paced around the room, panting hard. Michael yawned, rubbed his face, and checked his clock. His alarm was set for five o'clock because he was planning to get to his New York office early to prepare for an important meeting with out-of-town clients. He got up, pushed his feet into his slippers, and grabbed his robe. Roselle headed out of the room and down the stairs. She knew the drill. When they reached the basement, Roselle dove under the desk and began panting loudly again.

No one is quite sure why some dogs are afraid of thunderstorms. It could be the smell of the ozone from the lightning-ionized air, the drop in barometric pressure, the sounds of the storm assaulting the dog's exquisitely sensitive ears, or the static electricity hanging in the atmosphere. Whatever the cause, Roselle was terrified, and Michael sat up with her for more than an hour while the storm passed. Then they went back upstairs to bed.

Less than eight hours later, Roselle was under Michael's desk again, this time in Tower One of the World Trade Center. She dozed peacefully while Michael worked, prepping for the meeting. At 8:46 Michael heard a roaring explosion somewhere above. "Our tower started to groan and slowly tip to the southwest for over a minute," he said. "It felt like it tipped more than 20 feet." Michael said goodbye to David, a coworker, believing the building was going to crash to the street below and they were going to die. But the tipping stopped, and the building slowly righted itself.

Millions of pieces of burning paper began to rain down outside the windows. They heard screaming.

"Oh, my God!" David shouted. "We have to get out of here!" He quickly told Michael what he was seeing. And 78 flights of stairs were the only way out since elevators are off limits in emergencies.

Michael agreed they needed to get out, but he wanted to slow down and do it the right way: get the company guests out first, sending them down the stairs, and then close up the office and follow. "What David didn't understand was that I had information he did not have," said Michael. "While debris was falling, while David clearly saw flames, and while our guests were screaming and running for the exit, Roselle sat next to me as calm as ever. She didn't sense any immediate danger in the flames, smoke, or anything else going on around us. If she sensed danger, something I think she would have done if we were in imminent peril, she would have acted differently," Michael explained. "I used my complete trust in Roselle's judgment to determine that we could evacuate in a calm and orderly manner."

After the explosion and the violent tipping of the tower, Roselle had simply emerged from the desk to sit quietly by Michael, ready to do what was necessary. And this calmness from a dog who just a few hours earlier had been undone by a New Jersey thunderstorm!

Michael grabbed Roselle's harness. "Forward," he instructed Roselle. Forward is one of the first commands guide dogs learn. The verbal command is synchronized with a "forward" hand signal, a short motion with the right hand. They started out, and Roselle guided Michael carefully through the mess of papers, books, and office equipment strewn across the floor from whatever the impact was. The hallway was chaotic and buzzing with people.

Michael and Roselle made it to the stairwell and began their descent. He kept his right hand on the stair rail and held onto Roselle's leather guide harness with his left hand. They were 1463 stairs—78 flights—from ground level. They weren't alone, and the stairwell was brimming with panicked people anxious to get out.

Almost immediately Michael smelled a peculiar odor. It was faint, but he knew it was there even though no one else seemed to notice. After a few minutes of puzzling over the unusual odor, Michael figured it out. He told the people around him he thought he smelled burning jet fuel.

On floor 67, Michael heard someone shouting from above to make way for the injured. Soon a knot of people rushed by, surrounding and helping a woman who had been severely burned. Five minutes later shouts from above again asked people to move aside. Another burn victim was coming down.

A few minutes later, a woman nearby stopped and said she couldn't breathe. "We aren't going to make it out," she gasped. The group stopped to reassure the terrified woman. Without urging, Roselle nudged her hand, asking to be petted. The woman responded and even laughed a bit. She collected herself and was able to move on. Michael realized what Roselle had done, and he remembered the day he'd first met his dog. She'd entered the office at Guide Dogs for the Blind, walked over to where he was seated, and promptly given him a big kiss. There was something special about her doggie kisses. They were evidence of her lighthearted and loving spirit.

To keep his mind focused, Michael timed how long it took to go down each flight of stairs: about 20 seconds. There were two flights per floor, with ten steps in one flight and nine in the other. The odor of burning fuel was growing stronger. Michael started touching the fire doors on each floor as they passed, checking for heat.

The fumes, the burn victims, and the terror of the situation got to David. He suddenly stopped and sobbed, "Mike, we're going to die! We're not going to make it out of here."

Michael replied sternly, "David, stop that. If Roselle and I can go down the stairs, so can you!"

David was encouraged, and he soon moved to the front of their little group, walking a floor ahead of Roselle and Michael so he could shout back what he was seeing. He told Michael later that the stern rejoinder had snapped him back to his senses.

The group began to work as a team, watching out for each other and urging each other on. Trying to keep things upbeat, Michael made an offer to the group: "If the lights go out, Roselle and I are giving a half-price special to lead you out of here."

The stairwell began to heat up, and on floor 33 someone passed a water bottle up the stairs. Roselle was panting from the heat, but there wasn't enough water to slake her thirst. Just ahead, David called back to say he saw firefighters coming up the stairs. At the thirtieth floor the rescuers reached Michael. They were breathing hard because they were carrying close to 100 pounds of gear per man.

The first firefighter addressed Michael. "Hey, buddy. Are you okay?"

"I'm fine." Michael could tell the firefighter was petting Roselle, but it didn't seem like the time to give him the lecture about not petting a guide dog in harness, which meant the animal was in work mode.

"We're going to send somebody down the stairs with you," he said. Michael refused help, but the firefighter wasn't convinced until he saw David approaching. "Are you with him? Is everything okay?" he asked. David told him they were fine.

"Is there anything we can do to help you guys?" Michael asked.

"No," he replied. "You've got to go." With that the firefighter, the first in a long line of rescuers, shrugged his shoulders, resettling the tank on his back and turned to head upstairs. Before he left he gave Roselle one last pat. She kissed his hand, probably the last unconditional love he ever received.

As they got to the lower floors, the group's descent slowed as the stairwell grew more crowded. On the twentieth floor, Michael noticed the floor was getting slippery. *What was it from? Spilled water? Sprinklers? Sweat? Blood?* he wondered. Roselle panted heavily as they reached the tenth floor, but she continued do her job, walking and guiding Michael. Finally David called back that he had reached the first floor. Seconds later, when Michael and Roselle reached the first floor, Michael could hear the fire sprinklers going full blast. Roselle tried to drink some of the water off the floor, but Michael refused to let her in case there was some kind of contamination. He gripped her harness firmly, and they ran through the sprinklers. It was like a waterfall—more powerful than any shower he'd ever felt. "My poor dog was parched," Michael said, "but she did her job and took care of me."

When they emerged from the water, they were in the lobby of Tower One. It was chaos. People were shouting, telling the group where to run. Michael and Roselle left Tower One and ran through the concourse, an underground shopping center attached to the lobby. The shops were deserted. The group went up an escalator and outside onto the second floor plaza. For the first time since the chaos began, Michael and Roselle stepped into the sunlight. It was 9:45 in the morning. They stopped to catch their breath. It seemed like a lifetime since they'd first heard the explosion, but it had only been an hour—almost to the minute.

As they walked north on Broadway, David said he saw fire high up in Tower Two. Their first thought was that when their building tipped, the fire had jumped to the other tower. They couldn't think of anything else. David had a camera and stopped to take pictures of the fires while Michael tried to call his wife, Karen, on his cell phone.

"Get out of here!" someone suddenly yelled.

Michael and David heard a deep rumble, which quickly became a deafening roar. They heard glass breaking and metal tearing. David yelled that Tower Two was collapsing. The sound was like a waterfall of breaking glass or a freight train.

David screamed. They were only 300 feet from the towers.

Michael's first thought as he heard the collapse was a silent but anguished cry to God. "How could You get us out of the building only to have it fall on us?" As soon as he asked the question, he heard the answer as clearly as he had heard David. *Don't worry about what you can't control. Focus on running with Roselle, and the rest will take care of itself.* Immediately Michael felt a peace and a sense of protection. He was able to focus on Roselle and urge her on. He knew beyond a shadow of a doubt that God had spoken to him.

The noise of the falling tower became more intense and debris showered Michael and Roselle. They stopped to breathe. Suddenly a monstrous cloud of dust roared over and around them. It covered every inch of the two and nearly choked the life out of them. They moved forward again, and Roselle guided Michael perfectly. As they ran for their lives, Michael and Roselle sensed an opening on the right, and Roselle led Michael into it. She turned and then stopped abruptly, warning Michael that he needed to be ready for a change in their path. It was a flight of stairs, and it turned out to be the entrance to the Fulton Street subway station. They made their way down the stairs, all the time hearing the cacophony of noise as the collapsed building settled into its metal and glass grave.

At the bottom of the stairs was a small arcade. A woman nearby was crying and shouting that she couldn't see. Michael took her arm and said, "Please don't worry. I am blind but I have a guide dog named Roselle. She'll keep us both out of harm's way." The woman clutched Michael's arm and walked along with the two until her eyes cleared enough for her to see.

After a few moments of respite, a policeman came by and evacuated the station. Michael and Roselle climbed back up into the sunlight. The first thing David said was that there was no longer a Tower Two. All he could see was a pillar of smoke hundreds of feet high. The two men stood there for a moment and clasped hands. They walked east on Fulton Street, away from the World Trade Center. After walking for six or seven minutes, they heard the now familiar rumbling sound. The time was 10:29, and Michael realized that their tower—Tower One— was falling. After the noise stopped and another dust cloud passed, David said, "Mike, there is no World Trade Center anymore."

Michael took out his cell to call Karen. He got through this time. After confirming he was safe, they were silent. Then Karen told him what had been reported in the news about the terrorist attacks. They spoke for a few moments and then hung up.

As they made their way home, people wanted to talk. On the train from Penn Station to New Jersey, people wanted to know everything that had happened downtown, but talking was hard as shock settled in and Michael was overwhelmed by all that had happened. When he got home, Michael and Roselle had a joyous reunion with Karen.

Then Michael unharnessed Roselle, got her some clean, fresh water, and gave her a good brushing. She was covered in dust and debris. When that was done, she searched for her favorite toy, a Booda Rope Bone, even before she wanted to go outside to relieve herself. The family enjoyed a quiet meal from their favorite Chinese restaurant and then went to bed. This time Roselle slept peacefully.

Soon after the events of September 11, 2001, Michael and Roselle were invited to appear on *Larry King Live* to share their story. The public response threw them into the international limelight. Michael shared his unique survival story and 9/11 lessons of trust, courage, heroism, and teamwork. Michael and Roselle have become well-known as representatives of the strength of the human–animal bond.

In 2002 Roselle was honored by the American Kennel Club (AKC) with the ACE Award for Canine Excellence, recognizing "Dogs in the Service of Mankind." Roselle's name was read into the Congressional Record, and she was awarded a Certificate of Resolution by Guide Dogs for the Blind for displaying "exemplary courage, steadfastness, and partnership." She also was honored with the PDSA Dickin Medal, a British award recognized worldwide as "the animals' Victoria Cross" for conspicuous gallantry and devotion to duty. The last time the award had been given was in 1949.

Now in retirement, Roselle has an autoimmune blood disorder, possibly due to the inhalation of debris and dust from the World Trade Center disaster and collapse. She lives with Michael, Karen, and their two labs in a sunny house on the water near San Francisco Bay. And she is still handing out her special kisses.

13

Sophia in Wonderland

~≈~

But all lost things are in the angels' keeping, Love.

HELEN HUNT JACKSON

Angela's two dachshunds could often be found with their furry brown hindquarters and wagging tails sticking out of tortoise burrows. The holes, created by the gopher tortoise, dot the Surguines' five-acre property in Clermont, Florida.

The gopher tortoise is a land turtle about the size of a large dinner plate. It has a high, domed shell and weighs between 10 and 20 pounds. Its hind legs are large and stumpy while its front legs are flattened, shovel-like, to dig labyrinthine burrows in sandy soil. The tortoises can move quickly when they start excavating. "Sometimes I look out the window and see sand spraying out of a hole," said Angela. Gopher tortoise burrows are legendary—they can be up to 40 feet long and 20 feet deep.

The burrow openings are half-moon shaped with a curve at the top to fit the dome of the tortoise shell, and they are constructed with a separate entrance and exit. One tortoise may have multiple burrows, and since they can live to be 100 years old, that means one tortoise can do a lot of digging in a lifetime.

Gopher tortoises are a protected species. They reproduce slowly, and their habitat is threatened by development, so the tortoises must be professionally relocated before any land clearing or development takes place. Either that or you have to move your construction project somewhere else. This means the Surguine family didn't have the option of filling in or covering tortoise holes on their property.

The holes provided hours and hours of entertainment for Sophia and Zoe, the family's dachshunds. This breed of elongated, short-legged dogs was originally designed to hunt down burrow-dwelling animals such as badgers and rabbits. The name dachshund is from the German *dachs,* or badger, and *hund,* or dog. So Angela's two energetic little "badger hounds" were drawn to holes. The bodies of dachshunds, although long, are muscular, and the dogs have unusually large, paddle-shaped paws for efficient digging. Dachshund skin comes with a few extra folds so it is loose enough to flex and move while the dogs are tunneling in tight burrows. The breed typically has a deep chest to allow for increased lung capacity. A long snout and large nose provide a keen sense of smell for hunting prey.

Even though the dachshund has a specialized build for hunting, their comical appearance means they are sometimes the butt of jokes. They've been dubbed wiener dogs or sausage dogs, and people often dress them up in hot dog costumes on Halloween. H.L. Mencken once said that "a dachshund is a half-dog high and a dog-and-a-half long."

Sophia and Zoe loved to investigate by sticking their heads into the burrow entrances. They'd bark excitedly to announce their presence at tortoise burrow entrances. However, they had never gone all the way inside a burrow, and they had never run away. That's why it was strange when Sophia went missing.

Angela and her husband, Jim, were puttering around their yard on a Saturday in June. After a few hours of work in the 95-degree sunlight, they went inside to take showers and cool off. Angela noticed Zoe underfoot but didn't see her sister. *Something is wrong. This isn't like her. Zoe and Sophia always stay together.*

"Jim, where's Sophia?" she asked.

"I thought she came in with you," he replied.

Angela had a bad feeling. She walked the property, calling and looking for any sign of the little dog. She paced down the driveway and looked at the gate that opened onto the road. *She could have shimmied out that gate, and someone could have picked her up,* thought Angela.

The couple searched into the night but found nothing. Angela had a hard time sleeping as she thought about Sophia outside and unprotected among the bobcats and foxes that lived in the area. The next day Angela created lost dog flyers on colored paper and distributed them door-to-door around the neighborhood. She called the animal shelter three times, asking if a dachshund had been picked up or turned in. The search and flyers proved fruitless. No one had heard or seen anything about a lost dachshund. Sophia had vanished.

"She meant so much to me," Angela shared. "My family gave her to me for my birthday when she was just a little-bitty puppy."

Three days after Sophia disappeared, Angela put her grandson down for a nap and then went out back to check the pool cleaning equipment. She knew they'd want to go swimming in the afternoon. Angela loved being a caretaker of animals and people, and she often took care of her grandchildren while their parents were at work.

She was standing in the backyard looking at the pool when she heard a quiet moan. She froze, her heart pounding. *What is that?* She held her breath and listened carefully. *There it is. I hear it! Could Sophia be down in one of the tortoise holes?*

There was a tortoise hole on the other side of the pool, so Angela quickly went there. She got down on her hands and knees, leaned into the hole, and called Sophia's name. No response. Then she went around to every tortoise hole she could find, calling Sophia's name. Finally she went back to the hole by the pool and tried again. "Sophia! Sophia!" Suddenly she heard a muffled bark. She looked into the hole but couldn't see anything. And the bark was very faint, sounding like the dog was deep underground.

"I freaked out and started running back and forth," said Angela. "I went and got a shovel and started digging out the hole. I dug a little bit but couldn't get anywhere. The ground was too hard."

Her husband, Jim, was at work, so Angela called a 16-year-old neighbor boy to come and help her dig. They shoveled at the hole for an hour, but it started caving in and they realize they weren't making much progress. It was time to call for some professional help.

Angela called Jim, and then she considered calling the fire department. She decided to call animal control first. The assistant director for Lake County Animal Services arrived with an additional animal control officer, and they began to dig too. Neighbors and family, including Jim, arrived to help. Before long, a neighbor who operated a construction company arrived with his small Bobcat excavator.

As the digging progressed and the tortoise hole began to widen into a large pit, everyone listened for Sophia's bark so they would know where to dig. But she was silent. Angela was frightened. *What if the tunnels cave in and she suffocates? What if she gets scared of the noise and goes deeper?* Her son-in-law, Clint, took her aside. They went around the side of the house and prayed.

"I just had this feeling that God was telling me not to give up," Angela shared later. "I didn't feel Sophia was dead, and I couldn't give up."

Clint, a Baptist preacher's son, told her to put everything into God's hands.

By now the group had been digging for five hours in the 95-degree heat and high humidity. The pit had grown to 16 feet deep "and could fit ten people in it," said Angela. They had already taken out a tree and part of the garden. Jim felt the hole was getting too close to the swimming pool. Angela was torn; she knew some of the crew wondered if she'd really heard the dog's voice or if it had been wishful thinking. She knew people were starting to doubt.

"If she *was* alive, she's probably not anymore," someone said. The edges of the pit had caved in several times and the burrow had pretty much been destroyed.

Several people left for the night, and the rest went inside the house to cool off, have a drink, and get something to eat. Angela stayed outside. "I'm tenacious," she said. "I don't like to give up."

She was sitting in the hole when her husband came out to check on her. "What are you doing?" he asked.

"I'm going to find her, dead or alive," Angela stated.

She used her grandson's toy shovel from the sandbox and started digging. Jim went back into the house. Angela was digging all alone. Then their oldest daughter, Holly, stopped by after work to pick up her son. She came out to the yard to check on her mom. Taking off her tennis shoes, she jumped down in the hole. "Mom, are you sure she's down here?" Holly asked. *This is crazy,* she thought.

"Holly, yes. I am sure."

Holly knew very well the determination she heard in her mom's voice. She started helping her mom dig. The two women were working together silently when the other dachshund, Zoe, approached. With all of the chaos and noise of the search, she'd stayed in the background, quietly observing. Now it was quiet. She trotted to the edge of the pit and jumped down into the hole with Angela and Holly. When she jumped, the tags on her collar jingled together. Then the three of them heard something wonderful—frantic barking from somewhere underground.

The jingling of the tags must have reached Sophia's ears. Holly ripped off Zoe's collar and began to shake it. Sophia barked some more. Adrenaline shot through the women, and they yelled for help from the others. Angela noticed Sophia's barking was alternating between loud and faint. "It sounded like she was running back and forth in a tunnel underneath us."

The digging started again, this time with shovels. Angela was so afraid the dog would be buried, they decided to start digging with their hands. Clint was down on his knees digging when he yelled, "I'm through! I'm through!" Just then, a damp nose touched his fingers. He reached down through the dirt, grabbed Sophia's body, and pulled her up and out of the earth.

Angela fell to her knees, overwhelmed. "Thank You, Jesus!" she prayed out loud.

Sophia was covered in dirt. She shook herself and then ran to greet her sister Zoe, nose to nose. "The women all started bawling," Angela said.

The little dog looked pretty good for having spent three days 16 feet underground without food or water. The vet said later that the coolness of the underground tunnels had probably helped the dog survive.

Angela stayed up with her little badger dog all night. "I knew she was dehydrated, so I stayed up and made her drink water every half hour. I fed her cheese, and at 2:30, I cooked her some bacon." The next day they visited the vet, and Sophia got a clean bill of health—along with some all-natural medication for dogs who have been through traumas.

A dachshund getting stuck in a hole is not an uncommon story. Recently a dachshund in Bovey Tracey, England, was rescued by firefighters after being stuck in a badger hole for a day. He'd gone down the hole and then couldn't turn around to get out again. He was visible to rescuers, and they dug him out by the end of the day. Another dachshund, this one in New Hampshire, England, spent five days underground. Her owners searched the woods where she disappeared until they discovered the tunnel. Firefighters set up listening equipment and even sent a special snake eye camera underground. There was no sign of the dog. The owner used a pipe and funnel to try to detect noise in the tunnel and finally heard a faint whimper. Three hours later they recovered a hungry and thirsty Lucky.[1] He had been stuck eight feet underground.

In thinking about how the dog ended up so deep underground when she didn't usually go into holes, Angela figures that perhaps, with her head down in the entrance, she'd slipped down into the hole because of the steep incline and couldn't turn around to get back out.

Sophia has recovered from her underground adventure and is her usual sunny, loving self, although "she doesn't go into those holes anymore," said Angela. "Don't tell me dogs aren't smart."

While Sophia learned the perils of tortoise burrow exploration, Angela learned to listen carefully to God's voice. "My faith is always strong. When you have something you feel in your soul or heart, listen to that. That small voice is God trying to tell you everything's going to be okay."

And even though the gopher tortoise holes almost permanently swallowed her dog, Angela doesn't bear the tortoises any ill will. She continues to watch out for them, just like she does every living creature within her sphere. "Whenever I see a tortoise in the road, I always stop the car, get out, pick it up, and carry it to the side of the road," she said.

About three days after Sophia returned from the underground, Angela saw a good-sized tortoise walking across the back of the lawn. *That's probably the one who dug the hole,* she thought. And he was probably on his way to dig a new one.

Angela is the only child of a single mom, so "that's why I love my kids and my three grandkids so much." She loves having family around and taking care of everyone. She was the caregiver for her husband's father until he passed away. She also helped raise her husband's niece who had lost her mother when she was four years old. Besides dogs and cats, Angela has raised goats and chickens. "When the chickens are too old to lay eggs anymore, I just keep them as pets." She's currently keeping angora rabbits and plans to trim their fur and spin it to make yarn for the prayer shawls she likes to knit.

Angela reminds me of a female character in the C.S. Lewis book called *The Great Divorce.* Lewis is the author of the beloved children's series set in the mythical land of Narnia, as well as a book on theology called *Mere Christianity.* In *The Great Divorce,* he writes about an imaginary journey to hell and to heaven. He describes a woman in heaven surrounded by a great train of children, birds, and animals.

Angels dance and scatter flowers in front of her in honor. Two observers explain:

> "What are all these animals? A cat—two cats—dozens of cats. And all those dogs…why I can't count them. And the birds. And the horses."
>
> "They are her beasts."
>
> "Did she keep a sort of zoo? I mean, this is a bit too much."
>
> "Every beast and bird that came near her had its place in her love. In her they became themselves. And now the abundance of life she has in Christ from the Father flows over into them."

14

Toast and Hospitality

*A dog is the only thing on earth
that loves you more than you love yourself.*

JOSH BILLINGS

Kathi was crying on the sidewalk outside the animal shelter. Maximus, a golden-brown woolly mammoth of a dog, sat at her feet. He looked up at her with liquid-brown eyes, head cocked to the side, tail wagging slowly.

Up went a paw. He'd been driving Kathi crazy with the paw thing, leaving dusty paw prints on her work pants or scratching her bare leg with his thick dog claws. But this time it felt gentle, like a sympathetic friend patting her knee. "What am I going to do with you, Maximus?" she quavered.

Maximus was the best dog in the world who had come into her life at the absolute worst time. Kathi was in a very shaky marriage with a man who had been unemployed for two years. She felt rudderless at that point, like her life was falling apart. She and her husband didn't see eye-to-eye on much, and she was unhappy. She had two school-age kids she was desperately trying to shield from the flood of tension and conflict that was threatening to engulf the family. And she had recently taken on a sales rep job to help with finances. It was a tenuous time. She felt like she was walking a tightrope, tiptoeing over a raging river underneath. She was trying hard to keep it all together, and she lived consumed by worry.

Her lifeline during this trying time had been the church, especially her weekly Bible study. Her friends there heard her prayers for her husband, her marriage, and her sanity. They went out of their way to pray for her, to send her little notes, and to ask her how things were going. The group was a haven, a little island of warmth and peace in her stormy life.

The funny thing is that the group was studying hospitality, and as a group they had asked God to give them the gift of hospitality. *Ask, and you shall receive, right?* Kathi also prayed for God to help her show hospitality to the people in her life who needed it.

That night, lying in bed with her heart aching after another argument with an angry husband, she remembered that prayer. She wanted her life to become a warm and friendly place like the Bible-study group had become for her during a difficult time. Right there in bed she prayed and asked God to give her the gift of hospitality.

He answered the next day with 100 pounds of fur and tail-wag. His name was Maximus.

It was a beautiful spring evening. Easter was coming and Kathi was at church to rehearse with a group for the upcoming Easter presentation. She was getting a little frustrated because one of the actors, Dan, was late. Then he showed up with a huge dog. Absolutely huge, like a small pony. "Dude," Kathi said, "what are you doing bringing this dog to church?" She sat down in the room where they had been waiting and looked at the animal, a big furry bear of a dog panting happily. He came over and leaned against Kathi's leg and then put his head in her lap. Of course she melted. They got him a bowl of water and ended up going through their lines right there with Maximus standing next to her, his head in Kathi's lap. *What a giant goofy dog.* She rubbed his head and fingered his tail, and for a moment all her cares and worries drained away at the touch of his warm fur. He wiggled in happiness, his tail picked up in tempo, and she could swear he smiled a doggie smile. It was a spontaneous moment of life and love and joy. Just what she needed. A moment to forget her problems.

After rehearsal, Dan told the group the story. He worked as a bank teller at one of those little banks inside a grocery store. Maximus had sneaked into the supermarket and sat himself down in front of the meat counter. The employees found him and took him out, as a big furry dog wasn't exactly the most hygienic creature to be hanging out in a grocery store. But he came back in again. And again. The whole day, the employees would usher him out and he'd come right back in and sit in front of the meat counter, window shopping.

He obviously didn't belong to anybody. Finally, Dan's shift was over and it was time to go home. "I could tell the dog was loved by someone," he told us. "He was so happy and relaxed. He was just kind of hanging out, and I didn't want him to roam loose." So he led the dog out to his car. He couldn't take him home because he lived in a small, second floor apartment and he already had cats.

"What are you going to do with him?" Kathi asked, "because there's no way this dog can make it on the mean streets of San Jose." They lived in the Silicon Valley just south of San Francisco, and the area is a thicket of freeways and expressways, on ramps and off ramps. It's no place for a loose dog.

"I really have no plans," Dan said.

Okay, well at least I have a backyard, Kathi thought. *If nothing else, at least I've got a backyard.*

"Well, I'll take him," Kathi said. "What's his name?"

"He doesn't have a collar but I call him Maximus."

"Gluteus?" she said, because that was the only reference point she had for Maximus.

"No," he laughed. "Maximus, from the movie *Gladiator.*" The Russell Crowe movie had just come out, with Crowe starring as a tough

Roman general whose family is murdered, victims of treachery. Maximus is captured and thrust into the gladiator ring where he has to fight for his life.

This Maximus looked more like a lover than a fighter. Kathi figured she'd take him home for the night and then to the animal shelter the next day to see if anyone could help. He followed her out to the car and she opened the front passenger door. "Maximus, have a seat." she said. The car was warm from the late afternoon sun, and the dog's happy panting quickly filled up the inside of the car with a sort of mist composed of a mix of dog breath and musky fur.

Oh my goodness. What have I done? Maximus was lost. He had an owner somewhere. She just had to find out where he belonged. But for now, he needed her. For once she was thinking about something besides herself and her problems. It felt good.

Of course the kids fell in love with Maximus. Kimberly, eight, kept trying to feed him even though he was already stuffed, and Justen, ten, wanted to sleep with him. Maximus loved the attention, and they sat on the floor, crisscross applesauce, and Maximus kept laying his head on Kathi's lap. He was just a love. She knew he belonged to someone, but he was so sweet and joyful that she wanted to just enjoy him for a while. It was like a little vacation from real life, and her troubles melted away when she stroked his silky back and played with his floppy ears.

But then tomorrow came—too soon. Kathi knew she had to take him to the animal shelter. With her husband's unemployment, they could barely feed the kids, much less this big beast of a dog.

Late morning Kathi found herself at the animal shelter, Maximus at her feet. There was a problem: the animal shelter was chock-full of dogs. There was no room for him. But there was one more possibility. They scanned him for a microchip; if he had one, the shelter could trace the owner. And he did! They found a microchip, but it turned out to be inactive and not registered to any owner. Kathi looked down at the dog and felt her chest tighten with anxiety. *I don't know what to do.*

She explained how friendly and tame he was and that surely someone was looking for him. "I'm so sorry," the attendant said with a sad smile, "but I can't guarantee anything. When we're this full, the dogs are at risk. We can only promise that we will house him for three days. If no one claims him after three days, there's a chance he may have to be euthanized to make room for more dogs. Plus he's an older dog, and he's so big."

Before he finished his sentence, Kathi was already choking up. "Don't do the paperwork yet. Let me go talk to my husband and see if we can keep him," she said. She wheeled around and ran outside, where she now stood, weeping. She breathed in, trying to calm herself. She pulled out her cell phone and dialed her husband's work number. "We need to keep this dog," she told him.

"You're crazy," he said.

But Kathi couldn't just leave Maximus. She couldn't let him die. This dog had been a lifeline for her, a furry, wiggly injection of joy into a troubled life. He had lifted her outside herself for a little while, away from the problems that had consumed her. In just one evening he had brought a feeling of warmth and peace into their lives. She couldn't leave him to be put to sleep, just another dog in a building full of unwanted animals. She prayed, *God, please help me take care of this dog. Show me where to find him a safe place.*

She stood there, trying to decide what to do, sobbing quietly every once in a while, waiting. Kathi felt like she held Maximus's life in her hands, like he was suspended between life and death and it was all up to her. But she knew the reality, and she knew there was nothing else she could do at that point. She had to go back in there and surrender him. By this time Kathi was bawling. *I am a mess,* she thought.

As she went inside she heard someone screaming "Toast! Toast!" She looked up and saw a woman approaching. *Who is this crazy lady?* And there she was, a young woman, hanging over the reception desk and looking at Maximus. His whole body quivered a little and then froze. The stranger went down on one knee, and the dog ran around the end of the desk and dove toward her, tail wagging at hyper speed. She grabbed him around the neck and hugged him as if she would never let go. "Oh my!" she said, low and intense. "I thought you were gone forever." He was all over her face, nuzzling and licking. She was hugging him and crying. It was like when somebody's been gone for a really long time, like when a soldier comes home. Kathi could tell they belonged together. She could hardly believe it. It was like a last-minute reprieve from the gallows. The woman must have entered the building while Kathi was outside on the phone.

It was chaos for about ten minutes while the woman hugged her dog and cried. The woman had a friend with her, and her friend kept saying over and over, "You don't know how much this means." When everything settled down, her friend explained: She was a single woman and Toast was her only dog and a significant part of her life. The morning before she had been downstairs in the courtyard of her apartment building giving Toast a bath, dog collar off. Someone left the gate open and Toast (that was his real name; he was the exact color of a perfectly toasted piece of bread) had run away. The two women, along with a few other friends, had been up all night driving around looking for him. Kathi knew then the dog was very loved.

Tears ran down Toast's owner's face, and Kathi's too.

The woman looked up at Kathi. "Thank you. I thought I'd never see him again." She hugged Kathi and thanked her over and over.

Toast was wiggling in joy, back where he should be, in the arms of someone who cared for him.

"You'll never believe this." Kathi's voice trembled a bit. "I was praying for you before you came. The shelter is full, and I just couldn't leave him there. I didn't know what else to do, so I asked God to help me find you. Just now. Then you came." Kathi smiled through her tears. Kathi went on and told the story of how Toast had ended up with the group at church.

The dog's owner looked up at Kathi. "I can't believe it was a church," she said. "Are you a Christian?"

Kathi nodded but she felt embarrassed and awkward. *She thinks I'm a crazy woman,* Kathi thought.

"Well, you're the only Christian I've ever met who wanted to help me, not preach at me."

A couple of days later Kathi got back to church, and there was a package for her. Inside was a box of See's Candy addressed to Kathi and Dan, along with a note. "I can't believe the journey Toast took to get back to me: from grocery store to church to your house. I've always had a hard time believing in God, and I can't believe he ended up in church and that you guys took such good care of him. This was the first time in my life I've ever really prayed for anything."

"Toast and Hospitality" happened to Kathi Lipp, a writer and Christian speaker who lives in California. The Toast incident took place over a very short time period—just 15 hours or so—but it is still fresh in her memory as one of those pivotal moments when you get a chance to see God at work behind the curtain.

Years later, Kathi and her family adopted a puppy named Jake from the same animal shelter where Toast was reunited with his owner. Jake is a puggle (a beagle–pug mix) and is almost the same color as Toast. But he eats a lot less.

15

Tsunami Dog

*How beautiful on the mountains are the
feet of those who bring good news, who
proclaim peace, who bring good tidings.*

Isaiah 52:7

The once peaceful Indian fishing village now looked like a landfill with trash strewn all over. War correspondent Chris Tomlinson was covering the December 26, 2004, tsunami and its aftermath for the Associated Press (AP). He walked through the area with a translator to gather human interest stories.

Since the tsunami just a few days before, stories of death and destruction had saturated the media. A story had just come out of Thailand about a woman swept away by the tsunami, clutching her two children and keeping herself afloat by hanging on to a piece of debris. Struggling to keep her head above water, she was losing her grip and had to make a choice: let one of the children go and survive or hold on to both and perish. It was a heart-wrenching story. AP editors had requested more positive stories, so reporters in the Indian Ocean basin were on the lookout. After so much devastation and loss, people needed some good news. Stories that lifted spirits.

Chris, a 13-year veteran reporter covering wars and natural disasters, found one starring a scruffy yellow dog named Selvakumar. After several conversations with villagers who had lost everything, Chris began to piece together the threads of one particularly unbelievable story involving a family of five.

After the tsunami hit, Chris wrote two to three stories a day from the tsunami zone. A few days after the disaster, he walked into what was left of the village of Chinnakalapet. A tsunami is a series of waves caused by the displacement of a large volume of water. Because of the huge amount of water and energy involved, tsunamis can devastate coastal regions like those inhabited by fishing families in India. This tsunami was caused by an undersea megathrust earthquake off the coast of Sumatra, Indonesia. The earthquake registered between 9.1 and 9.3 on the Richter scale, the second largest earthquake ever recorded on a seismograph. It lasted 8 to 10 minutes. More than 230,000 people were killed in 14 countries.

In Chinnakalapet, palm trees 25 feet high were crowned with trash picked up and then left by the waves. The geography of the area had changed. Newly formed sand dunes had swallowed up some of the small concrete buildings. The houses that survived the angry waves were full of sand. Modest huts had simply disappeared, washed away by the powerful waves. The statues in the Hindu temple had been knocked over and shattered, while the brightly painted pillars that held up the roof had collapsed. A large Ganesh (elephant god statue) was destroyed. A local ashram or religious center frequented by American visitors had responded to the emergency by opening up a field kitchen to feed the villagers. A tent city sprouted up high atop a hill to shelter the now homeless fishermen and their families.

Buildings had been destroyed and possessions swept away, but even worse, lives had been lost. Approximately 20 percent of the village's inhabitants had been killed by the tsunami. Grief reigned.

Chris first heard about the extraordinary dog from villagers, and then he confirmed the story by tracking down the dog's owners in the makeshift camp. He met with the family's mother and said, "Please tell me what happened." The mother's husband was a fisherman, and together they had three sons, ages three, five, and seven. They also had a skinny yellow dog named Selvakumar. The dog was closest to the seven-year-old boy named Dinakaran (pronounced *deena-karen*). The dog had joined the family when Dinakaran was just two years old, and he and the boy had bonded. He followed the boy to school, went home to wait, and then at the end of the school day trotted back to walk Dinakaran home.

The family had little extra money and couldn't afford special food, so Selvakumar was expected to scavenge for himself. Though they loved the dog, like the other village pets it subsisted on fish scraps left over from the catch, with an occasional rat or table scrap as a treat.

In India, fishermen belong to a "low" caste. The people are looked down upon and separated from the surrounding society. They tend to live in ramshackle fishing camps near the beach. Most live in mud huts, but if the ground is firm enough, sometimes a concrete building is erected with government help. In this village, the fishermen's huts were strung out along the beach at sea level, about 25 yards from the water. Behind the village was a steep hill that could be climbed to reach the highway that ran along the coast through the state of Tamil Nadu. The wealthy people lived at the top of the hill away from the fishing families.

Since the tsunami, the family was living in a camp with others from the devastated village. They were on the other side of the highway up on the hill. "The people didn't understand what a tsunami was or if it was coming back," said Chris. In most cases, the fishermen and their families had, at most, an elementary school education. They were relying on the charity of the ashram and waiting for government officials to show up. They were all trying to figure out what they were going to do.

As Chris talked to the woman with the translator's help, he watched Dinakaran play with the dog. There was an obvious, close bond between the two. They were best buddies. Dinkaran's mom began the story.

On the day of the tsunami, everyone heard a strange ruckus down toward the water. People were yelling and screaming. The family went outside and headed toward the cement block community center, the father in the lead. He climbed on the roof to see what was happening while his wife and the three boys waited below.

He saw something he didn't understand. The ocean had pulled back and left the beach bare, exposing sand at levels he'd never seen before. Because it had happened so suddenly, there were fish stranded on the sand and people from the village were running around gathering them up.

Dinakaran's dad then saw a strange sight out in the distance that strangled his breath. A monstrous wave was rolling in. He screamed down to his wife, "Run! Run!" as he pointed up the hill. There wasn't time for anything else. He jumped down as his wife was picking up the three-year-old and the five-year-old. Like the woman in Thailand, she couldn't hold on to all three. She ran, along with her husband, calling for Dinakaran to follow.

But he didn't.

As seven-year-olds do, Dinakaran headed for the safest place he knew—under his bed. Instead of following his family and the other villagers up the hill to safety, he ran to the family hut and hid. Then the tsunami rolled in and destroyed the village.

In the ensuing confusion and chaos, Dinakaran's parents assumed he had followed them and was climbing the hill somewhere close by, along with the rest of the village. But after moments passed and he didn't show up, they panicked. His mom was crying, sure the angry ocean had swallowed up her son. Dozens of people were missing.

Like Lazarus unexpectedly emerging from the tomb with the town watching, Dinakaran showed up alive, dog in tow. When things had finally settled down at the top of the hill and families sorted themselves out, neighbors had come across Dinakaran and led him to where his family was. His mother wept with joy as Dinakaran explained what had happened. He said he'd run home and hid under his bed. The dog had followed. "The dog came in, bit into his clothing, and started dragging and pulling on the kid to get him to leave the house," said Chris. The boy told Chris that the dog had grabbed him by the collar. "He left the house with the dog herding him like he was a sheep. The dog herded the kid up the hill along with everyone else. He was nipping at the boy's heels while they were running up the hill."

His mother had wept with joy. Their scruffy, yellow, scrap-eating dog had done something she could not—save her son from destruction.

Chris had a hard time believing the story, his war correspondent's natural skepticism kicking in. "If I'd not heard it from several different people I wouldn't have bought it," he said. "But I did ten interviews for this one. I wanted to make sure I had independent witnesses." And he did. Everyone described the scene the same way: Selvakumar had herded his boy up the hill, snapping at his heels.

"I think the dog knew instinctively that his herd was running in one direction, and the little boy wasn't. He knew something was wrong," Chris added.

Chris had seen a lot during his many years reporting in war and disaster zones, and he describes himself as jaded. "I'm not used to happy endings and that sort of thing," he said. After he wrote the story, he didn't have time to sit back and reflect on the tsunami dog. He filed it, and then went on to the next story. But the story resonated with people, a reminder that in the midst of an overwhelming tragedy, there can be good news. And Chris got to deliver it.

The story of the tsunami dog flashed around the world and made a bright spot in the very dark news coming out of the tsunami zone. Out of all the stories Chris wrote in his career as a war correspondent, this one was the most read. Chris said, "It was at the top of Yahoo News for three days, and appeared in just about every language newspaper in the world. People really loved this story because after four days of tragedy, this one good news story was released."

Strangely enough, Chris is not an animal lover. "I'm allergic to dogs," he said. "If I touch one and then touch my face, my eyes swell shut. I'm not a dog person or a cat person or any kind of animal person because they make me ill." But Chris is a people person. He now lives in Texas and serves as managing editor of the *Texas Observer,* a non-profit investigative journalism magazine based in Austin.

He is at work on a book and film about racism and bigotry in Texas and in the seven ethnically influenced wars he's covered around the world. He may not care much about dogs, but Chris cares. Deeply.

16

When Ohio Came Alive

~≈~

Love means to love that which
is unlovable, or it is no virtue at all.

G.K. Chesterton

The dog always reminded Mary of an old street bum who had nobody to love him. Every day she took a walk around the neighborhood. And every day she saw the chow chow lying in the middle of the
street. She always gave him wide berth. Even from a distance she could
see the leaves and branches tangled in his bushy red fur. His matted red
mane had grown so long that she figured he could hardly see. And his
eyes were blank, dark pools of misery.

The street belonged to the dog, and the neighbors learned to drive
around him. Every day when Mary turned the corner, she hoped to
see a transformed dog. *Maybe this is the day they will have groomed him.*
But it never happened. "I must have walked by this dog every day for
a couple of years," said Mary. "I just got to where I couldn't stand it
anymore." She had to do something, but she didn't know what. So she

began to pray. She enlisted her husband, Allen, to join her in prayer. "I asked God to allow me to do something in this dog's life, to help this dog some way. I knew if I called the dog pound, they'd come get him and put him to sleep," said Mary. "That's not something I could even think about, but I didn't know what else to do."

Mary had always noticed people and animals in need, and she tried to help however she could. One local man, a well-known character named Eddie, had made a huge impact on her. She'd seen him around town for years. He wore a suit, tie, and hat, all filthy, and always had a cigarette hanging out of his mouth. He was friendly and talked to everyone.

One year Mary was involved with setting up a Thanksgiving dinner for the homeless. At the last minute, the location was changed due to the number of people planning to attend. The organizers worked hard to spread the word about the change. The night of the dinner, Mary was driving home when she saw Eddie walking on the opposite side of the road. She heard a voice in her head say, "Tell the man where his Thanksgiving dinner is." She kept driving. The closer she got to home, the louder the voice got. The same thought kept running through her head. Finally, it was like thunder: *Tell the man where his Thanksgiving dinner is!*

Mary gave in. She turned the car around, found Eddie, stopped alongside, tooted her horn, and motioned for Eddie to open the door and get in. Eddie jumped inside, and they exchanged names. Eddie said, "I'm trying to find my Thanksgiving dinner, but I can't find it anywhere."

Laughing to herself, Mary answered. "I know exactly where it is, and I'll take you." She drove him to the new location for the dinner. Just before he got out of the car, Eddie looked at her and said, "God sure is good, ain't He?"

She never forgot that night or what happened when she listened and responded to that inner urging she was sure was from God. She thought of the Eddie incident as an assignment from God. It was the same with the dog in the street. "It was one of those things you just know you have to do," she said.

One day a friend came to visit. She was a dog lover, and Mary invited her for a walk. "I wanted to see what her reaction to the chow chow would be," Mary shared.

They headed out, turned the corner, and "sure enough, there was that old dog." This time they walked within several yards of him.

"What's this?" said her friend, shocked. She dropped to one knee and tried to talk to the dog that was lying quietly in the middle of the street as usual. He looked at them through the matted fur above his eyes but gave no sign that he wanted to be approached.

The dog's lack of friendliness could be attributed in part to his extreme neglect. But reserve also runs in the breed. Chow chows are known to be very territorial and to take their job of guarding their owner and owner's property very seriously. One online dog owner's guide describes the breed as "naturally suspicious of strangers and very territorial." Chows have a serious, dignified demeanor and don't usually give people a warm welcome.

Chows are an ancient breed, originally developed in Mongolia about 4000 years ago. In China, the chow chow is called *Songshi Quan,* which means "puffy lion dog." The chow was used by the Chinese as an all-around working dog for hunting wolves, sable, and pheasant, along with herding, pulling carts, and guarding property. The chow was also used to provide fur and as food. In the late 1800s, chows arrived in England on merchant ships. The breed's name originated from "chow-chow," a slang term at the time for small goods and knickknacks imported from China.

Mary's friend wanted to know which house belonged to the dog's owner. Mary pointed it out and said, "If you'll go with me, I'll talk to that lady." Mary didn't really know the woman; they'd only said hello a few times in passing. She was nervous. *How will this woman react when I ask her about this dog? What am I going to find?*

Before they approached the house, Mary decided to pray again. In the driveway, the two women prayed and asked God to guide their words. They were angry about the dog's condition, but they wanted to approach the woman in a sincere, caring fashion. Their anger subsided, and they felt they could talk rationally and calmly with the dog's owner.

Mary took a deep breath, knocked on the door, and a woman answered.

"Is that your dog out there on the street?" Mary asked, looking into the woman's eyes.

She nodded.

"Don't you like that dog?" Mary's voice quivered a bit.

"I hate that dog!" the woman said, her face twisted in pain. "That dog belonged to my husband. He left me, he left the kids, and he left that dog. I *hate* that dog." She went on to explain that besides the bad memories the dog stirred up, she had two little girls and was afraid for their safety. The dog reacted meanly when the girls approached him. She also added that the chow was 11 years old.

Mary felt sad. "Would you consider letting me have the dog?" She couldn't believe what had just come out of her mouth. She'd never had a mad dog before. *What am I doing?* she wondered.

"You can have him," the woman said. "But he won't come to you. He's mean. He won't let you touch him."

But agreement was all Mary and her friend needed to hear. They hurried back to Mary's house, grabbed a leash, and returned to confront the dog.

The owner came out to watch. "He's not gonna let you put that on him."

"Oh, yes he will," said Mary's friend.

And he did. This dog who looked like an angry lion lay still and allowed himself to be leashed. But getting him to move was another story altogether. "We dragged him back to the house," Mary said. "I mean, we physically dragged him. He was not walking. He would not come."

The women managed to get him back to Mary's house by alternately pulling on the leash, dragging him, and pushing on his haunches.

They tied him to a tree outside and then went inside to tell their husbands what they'd done. Mary's friend's husband said, "Oh no. No! We have enough rescue dogs. We are *not* taking another dog home."

Then Mary's husband, Allen, chimed in. "We aren't taking it either."

"We hadn't had a dog in ten years, and we weren't looking for one,"

Mary said. "And I have always tried to do things the way my husband wants. I rarely countered him. But this time was different." Mary looked at Allen, her eyes blazing. "We…are…going…to…take…this…dog!" Mary declared. "Remember how we prayed?"

Allen looked at Mary, eyebrows raised. He didn't say a word.

Mary scrounged up two pairs of scissors and a big trash can. The two women went outside with their gear. The dog was still lying quietly outside under the tree. They got to work on the chow. Mary took the back end and started cutting away the filthy, matted fur. It was at least six inches long and very thick. Mary's eyes filled with tears as she cut away dried fecal matter, burrs, and knots. She felt like she was shearing a neglected lion. Her friend took the front end. The dog snapped and snarled at her, but she soothed him with quiet words. "She has a real way with animals," Mary noted.

Then Mary noticed something strange. The dog had a bluish-black tongue. Her friend explained that this was a unique characteristic of the chow. An old fable says that when God was painting the sky blue, he spilled a few drops as he worked. The dog followed along, licking up the spilled paint. From that day forward, the chow chow had a blue tongue.

It took a couple of hours, but slowly, surely, the matted coat came off. "We clipped his entire body," Mary said.

Then came a beautiful sight. The chow stood up, stretched, and shook himself. Dust and clipped fur sprayed in all directions. His skin rippled and twitched as fresh air touched his skin for the first time in many, many years. The blank look left his eyes, and he seemed to look around with fresh energy, taking in his new yard. Then he began to dance with joy.

"That dog came alive! He started jumping around, and so did we," Mary exclaimed. "It was the most wonderful thing—to see that dog free of all those years of neglect." They called their husbands out to enjoy the scene.

To go along with his new look and his new life, Mary wanted a new name for the dog. His old name, Cleveland, didn't fit him anymore.

Allen was responsible for naming any animals in their household, so he thought about it for a few minutes, and came up with a new name: Ohio. In Japanese, Ohio is an informal way to say "good morning." And from that morning on, everything changed for Ohio.

First, he needed a real grooming—more than Mary and her friend could provide with dull kitchen scissors. Chow chows are popular for their lush coat. With their regal manner and thick, furry mane, they look like lions. As puppies, they look like walking teddy bears. But their coats aren't easy to maintain. Grooming is a daily necessity to prevent matting. Once or twice a year they shed much of their coats, producing trash bags full of fur.

The very next day Mary loaded Ohio in the back of her pickup truck and headed to a local groomer. She got him inside, but Ohio was frightened. He snarled and threatened to bite. The groomer muzzled him, but he tore right out of it. The groomer asked Mary to take the dog and leave.

She went to a second groomer and the scene was replayed, even down to chewing off the muzzle.

The third groomer, however, hit it off with Ohio. She talked to him, approached him quietly, and calmed him enough to clip off the rest of his coat and even up Mary's homemade job. Chows have a thick undercoat that helps insulate the skin from heat and cold. Without regular grooming, this hair packs down next to the skin and traps dirt, heat, and moisture. Fresh air can't reach the skin. In addition, the matted hair irritates and rubs against the dog's sensitive skin. In the warm Southern California neighborhood where Ohio lived, he must have been absolutely miserable.

With Ohio neatly shorn, the next stop was the veterinary clinic for an evaluation of his health. The vet could tell immediately that Ohio wasn't going to cooperate, so he sedated the chow. After his examination, Mary was shocked when the vet came back with the results: Ohio was surprisingly healthy.

"And that began our journey," said Mary. "After two years of making a detour around him in the street, this dog touched my heart.

Nobody loved him. I was determined that Ohio was going to know that he was worthy of love."

Ohio settled into his new home. His coat began to grow back, and his aloofness and snarly attitude melted away. Mary took him on walks, practicing the heel and sit commands. His gait took on a happy, confident bounce. She groomed him every day, and he came to enjoy the hours she spent on him. He regained his lion look. And he ate well. "When we had a steak, he had a steak," said Mary. "He was worthy of the best I could do for him."

Allen built him a beautiful doghouse, insulated and drywalled with a detachable peaked roof for cleaning. The floor was padded and carpeted. Mary painted the doghouse green. She also painted a faux window with yellow café curtains on the front, and a white crisscross Dutch door on the little door. An oval rag rug served as a welcome mat. "Ohio" was painted in elegant white letters over the door.

Yet something still bothered Mary. Even though Ohio seemed happy in his new home, if she released him from the leash on their walks he would run away and return to his old home. "It was kind of hurtful," said Mary. "His old owner hated him, and I was trying to help him. He kept running back to the pigpen." At certain moments it seemed his chow chow loyalty kicked in so he returned to his old familiar haunt in the middle of the road.

But Mary kept at it, and slowly, slowly Ohio accepted his new home and the woman who poured out her love. He left the old life behind like so much matted fur and embraced love, joy, and his carpeted doghouse.

He lived a long and happy life. So did Eddie, the homeless guy, who lived to the ripe old age of 92, enjoying many more Thanksgiving dinners. And Mary? She is always looking for her next assignment from God.

It's hard to know what to do if, like Mary, you come across a dog who clearly hasn't been properly cared for. According to "Unchain Your Dog," an organization dedicated to educating people about how to help chained-up or neglected dogs, Mary did the right thing by talking to the dog's owner in a nonconfrontive manner. It's important to be constructive, not critical. Offer to help by walking the dog or finding the dog another home. If necessary, gently educate the owner so he or she will think of the dog in a new light—as a living creature who needs love, attention, and care. One simple way to do this is to place educational brochures and flyers on the owner's porch. If the dog is too thin, infested with parasites, or has matted hair, you can say, "I've got some extra flea treatment at home. May I drop some by?" or "I like working with dogs. May I come over sometime and groom your dog?" If the owner is unresponsive, if the dog is consistently without food, water, or shelter, or if the animal looks sick or infested with parasites, it's best to call the local animal control office, Humane Society, or sheriff's department.

Mary put what she learned from Ohio in a little booklet called *The Gospel According to Ohio.* "That booklet has gone all over the world," she said. "When God points something out to us that needs attention, we need to trust Him enough that we'll take the assignment. The rewards from that assignment are far-reaching."

17

You Can't Catch Me

*Faithfulness lives where love
is stronger than instinct.*

PAUL CARVEL

The phone kept ringing. Santa Cruz Animal Services heard the same report over and over again. "There's a dog sleeping by the side of the highway, but when we stopped to try to catch him, he ran away." Field Supervisor Todd Stosuy sighed. Trying to catch the dog they'd nicknamed Highway Man was becoming a regular part of his morning routine. It wasn't just the man hours, although those were beginning to add up. It was his frustration over repeated failures to bring the dog into the safety of the shelter.

It all started back in January when a call came in that a dog was sleeping directly underneath the brown Santa Cruz Harbor sign on Highway One between 41st Avenue and Soquel Avenue. Highway One is a jewel of a state highway that runs along the Pacific Coast of California. Also known as the Pacific Coast Highway, it starts down in

Orange County and runs up along Los Angeles and the upscale beach towns of Santa Monica and Malibu. From there, it stretches from Ventura to San Luis Obispo, then up to Monterey and Santa Cruz.

After that very first phone call, Todd and his crew went out a couple of times to try to catch the dog. Most dogs aren't that hard to catch. They either run home or let themselves be cornered and leashed. But Highway Man was different. He refused to be caught. Every time they went out to capture him the dog eluded them and ran into the woods until they gave up.

Passing drivers stopped eight to ten times a day to try to help the dog. As they drove down Highway One, drivers saw a dog sleeping on the shoulder of a very busy road near an industrial complex. Highway Man had a cute face: black with a white stripe that ran down between his eyes and onto his muzzle, encircling his nose. His ears were perky, flopped over at the top and slightly crooked, his left ear higher than his right. He had big, intelligent brown eyes and golden eyebrows. Again and again people saw him, stopped, tried to lure him to their cars, and ended up fruitlessly chasing him around the highway. They didn't know Highway Man lived there in that spot under the brown sign. And he wasn't about to leave.

On one of the attempted captures, Todd discovered a homeless encampment in the bushes behind the spot where Highway Man hung out. "It looked like a comfortable home," said Todd. "There were tarps strung up to form a roof, sides, and a door." The makeshift camp was well camouflaged, and Todd could tell that someone had used it for sleeping and for cooking. But now it was empty. Whether the resident had moved, been arrested, or taken ill, the camp had been abandoned. And so had Highway Man.

They city of Santa Cruz is a Bohemian beach town known for its stunning forests of coastal redwoods, a harbor populated with sea otters and sea lions, and a popular beach boardwalk. The boardwalk is California's oldest amusement park and home to the beloved Giant Dipper, a 1924 wooden roller coaster. The beautiful beaches, mild weather, and laid-back atmosphere attract transients to Santa Cruz, so the homeless encampment was no surprise to Todd. But homeless people usually didn't leave their dogs behind.

"A lot of transients have dogs or cats," said Todd. "The majority are really good pet owners. They take their animals with them everywhere; they're with them 24/7, and the animals are usually fed before they feed themselves." Highway Man looked to be well fed and healthy so whoever owned him had taken good care of him.

But Highway Man was determined to wait by the road for his owner. Every day he took up his position under the brown sign, curled up, and waited. And waited. When Animal Services showed up, he ran into the woods and hid. When they left he'd return and wait some more.

Loyalty and intelligence run through Highway Man's bloodlines. He is an Australian cattle dog mix, a breed of herding dog developed in the mid-1800s in Australia for moving livestock across rugged terrain. The breed's ancestors include the dingo, a wild native Australian dog, Scotch Merle collies, and the bull terrier. Australian cattle dogs are known for their athleticism, courage, stamina, and intelligence. The breed ranks tenth in a list of the most intelligent breeds, published by Stanley Coren's *The Intelligence of Dogs*.[1] Australian cattle dogs are also known for their staunch loyalty.

One remarkable Australian cattle dog named Blue stayed next to his 83-year-old owner after she took a fall while on an evening walk in Fort Myers, Florida, and couldn't get up. Suddenly Blue ran off into the dark, and she heard growling and snarling. People realized later that an alligator had emerged from a nearby canal and Blue had attacked, suffering dozens of serious lacerations in the fight. When the owner's family returned from an outing, Blue met them at the car and led them to his owner. He recovered with some serious battle scars to show for his courage. Another Australian cattle dog named Molly Minogue fell out of a pickup truck in a rural area of Australia. She stayed by the road awaiting her owners. Seven days later, they found her.

Probably the most well-known example of canine loyalty was a Japanese dog named Hachikō, an akita adopted by a University of Tokyo professor. Every day Hachikō greeted his owner at the nearby Shibuya train station. One day the professor suffered a cerebral hemorrhage and died while at the university. Hachikō continued to go to the train station to meet the professor. Every day he waited for the professor to get off the train; every day he went home disappointed. Even after he found a new home, Hachikō often ran away and went back to the station. Commuters became fond of him and brought him food and dog treats. He became a familiar figure at the station and continued his routine for nine years until his death. His legendary faithfulness inspired the country and a bronze statue was erected in his honor at Shibuya Station. Books, movies, and television shows have recounted Hachikō's story. Hachikō was an akita, not an Australian cattle dog, but Highway Man's faithfulness to his absent owner echoed Hachikō's. Both dogs used wit and courage to hold on and wait.

Because Highway Man chose to wait by the side of a busy road, though, he was creating a serious hazard to himself and motorists. With passersby regularly trying to catch him, Todd was afraid it wouldn't be long before either the dog was hit by a car or a dog-chaser was hit by a car.

The next step for Animal Services was a humane catch trap. The live animal trap was baited and when a dog stepped in, his paw would hit a lever that snapped the door shut behind him. It almost always worked.

The crew washed the trap completely down to get rid of any human scent and worked at camouflaging the trap. At one point Todd bought a lamb's neck from the grocery store and rubbed it all over the trap so it smelled "really, really intense." Over the course of a month, they tried different locations and tricks to make the trap attractive, leaving bait trails of food usually very attractive to dogs. But Highway Man seemed to know what was going on and never nibbled on the food in the bait trail leading up to the trap, never mind the actual bait in the trap. "He could sense the trap was something we were doing, and he knew well enough to stay away from it," Todd said.

Next they tried tranquilizers. The crew baited some tuna fish more than 100 yards away from the trap so the dog wouldn't associate the two. Just recently they had used the exact same tranquilizer variety and dosage to knock out some huge Italian mastiffs and rottweilers at a renegade dog breeder's place in Boulder Creek. There had been more than 80 dogs to round up, and Todd had led the group that tranquilized the dogs and successfully captured them. The breeder was later convicted of animal cruelty. The crew was confident this tactic would work.

Success seemed near. Highway Man went for the tuna. The crew watched him eat and then lie down in the woods and fall asleep. They waited for a while, but when they finally approached the dog jumped to his feet and took off. Again. "I don't know how he did it," said Todd. "Adrenaline maybe? He'd ingested enough tranquilizer to knock out a 100-pound rottweiler mix. And this dog was only 40 to 50 pounds."

The next strategy involved involved a human dragnet. First, the California Highway Patrol closed down the highway. Then a group of ten people, made up of Highway Patrol officers, Animal Services officers, and animal care people, formed a large circle and slowly moved in to surround the dog and cut off his escape routes. "It sounds kind of like Keystone Cops," said Todd, "but it's usually an effective method because with that many people you can close the perimeter and find a spot where you can catch the dog with a Snappy Snare or a leash." But that didn't work either. Highway Man eluded capture, using the woodsy terrain to disappear into.

Failure was not an option for Todd. He was becoming increasingly frustrated. "We spent so much time trying to catch this guy. But at the same time, he seemed content to be living on the side of the road. He doesn't have a family. But he could very easily walk out on the highway and get killed or cause a horrific accident."

What finally got Highway Man in the end was a completely camouflaged trap. Todd and the crew covered the metal trap with leaves and pine needles so it looked like a cave. Highway Man finally took the bait, and the door shut. They had him.

The final tally? Highway Man: 80; Animal Services: 1. When Todd looked back at the records over the past couple of months, he realized they'd made 80 official Animal Service visits to capture the dog, including several highway closures and tranquilizer attempts. It was by far the most challenging dog capture case he'd ever had.

The repeated capture efforts never once drove Highway Man away. Each time he waited in the woods, hiding, until Animal Services left. Then he'd return to his spot on the shoulder of Highway One and wait under the sign.

Once Highway Man was safely in custody at the county animal shelter, the next question was what to do with such a super-intelligent, street-smart dog who seemed to want to have nothing to do with people. Although Highway Man had been his nemesis, Todd had become attached to the dog over the past few months. He admired the dog's tenacity and will to survive. But there was a problem. "Because of his antisocial behavior, he wouldn't normally have been considered a candidate for adoption."

Highway Man's life hung in the balance, and his chances didn't look good. A major setback occurred when the children of the director of the animal shelter visited the shelter and Highway Man became so frightened he lost control of his bladder and bowels. The next day, Highway Man's case was reviewed by the shelter's Humane Animal Review Team (HART), a committee formed to seek solutions for problem animals. Everyone wondered if Highway Man would ever recover because the dog had displayed such intense fear. The consensus was mixed on the dog's potential for rehabilitation, but a shelter employee named Gustavo Cabrera argued strongly that Highway Man should be given a second chance.

That's when Rena Cochlin stepped in. A longtime provider of foster care for dogs and cats who needed new homes, Rena had successfully fostered 70 dogs. A dance teacher at the University of California, Santa Cruz, she has three dogs of her own and uses them to help rehabilitate dogs who have been mistreated or neglected.

Rena visited Highway Man at the shelter. He cowered in the back of his enclosure. "I made several visits," Rena said, "and pretty soon I could sit next to him. Then I started to touch him, and I felt a rapport with him." When she brought one of her own dogs to visit, there seemed to be a breakthrough. Highway Man immediately warmed up to Rena's 15-year-old dog and happily accompanied them for a friendly visit in a different enclosure.

Rena saw something positive in the dog and agreed to take him home for foster care. At first he stayed out of sight, hiding in Rena's house. He had to be fed alone in a separate room and was afraid of any movement. But with time, Rena's loving care, and the companionship of her three very calm dogs, Highway Man's fear and shyness melted away.

"He is a happy dog and loves to run and play with other dogs," said Rena. She takes him out for long walks in the fields near her house and to outings at a dog park. He's more comfortable with people now. "He likes to be petted, and he loves to lie next to me. When I'm driving the car, he comes and nudges his face against mine."

One day on a walk near the university, a man rode by on a bicycle. Highway Man went crazy, crying, pulling on his leash and trying to follow the bike. And that was just the first time. Every time he saw a man on a bike, he became extremely agitated. After several bicycle episodes, Rena changed her response. Instead of giving verbal reassurance, she stopped and physically held him. "I embraced him and said, 'You don't have to worry. I'll be here to take care of you and you'll never be left again.' He knew I was comforting him, and he settled down much faster," said Rena. "But it's so painful. One can assume, although one can never know, that since he was living in a homeless encampment that his owner rode a bicycle."

Highway Man's shyness continues to dissipate as he recovers from his ordeal on the highway. In the next year or two, he'll be ready for a new home. "There's just something about him," said Rena. "A lot of people are attracted to him. He has beautiful eyes, and when you look at him you feel a kinship with him."

Rena's life has changed since Highway Man moved in. "I didn't realize what a project he was going to be," she said. "But I love watching him improve from a frightened dog slinking around to becoming more social and showing a great deal of love. That's the joy of fostering. Every time I start with a new dog I think I'm crazy, and then after a week I think it's wonderful."

Not long ago, Rena invited Todd and his wife over for dinner. Highway Man remembered Todd and stayed away at first. "My presence scares him," said Todd. But by the time dinner was over, the dog quietly approached Todd, put his head in his lap, and allowed Todd to pet him.

This time there was no leash, no snare, no tranquilizers, and no trap. Just a man and a dog—once enemies, now friends.

Highway One is safer now, but it's also a lot less exciting.

Before he began working in Animal Services, Todd Stosuy wanted to be a police officer. He earned a degree from Rutgers University in New Jersey, a university with an international reputation for academics. But after a couple of internships with police departments he realized the job wasn't for him. He started working with People for the Ethical Treatment of Animals where he conducted investigations into animal abuse and neglect across the country. He met animal control officers and soon realized he could be a cop and work with animals. Animal Services officers used to be portrayed as cruel dog catchers, but their image has been changed, and the public is beginning to perceive them as law enforcement officers with a legitimate mission to stop animal cruelty and abandonment. Stosuy is also vice president of the National Animal Control Association (NACA). However, not everyone understands their mission. "In some places you're still just the dog catcher," Todd said. A recent highlight in Todd's career was the coordination of animal rescues during three major wildfires in Santa Cruz County. He is credited with evacuating approximately 875 animals! Not bad for a humble dog catcher.

Ordinary Dogs

≈≈

*He's got his dog trained so that it only
does it on newspapers. The trouble is
it does it when he's reading the blasted things.*

HONORÉ DE BALZAC

A chubby bulldog surprised his owner when he ran away and jumped into a pond. The dog swam to the middle, grabbed a crumpled floating bag, and then towed it back to shore. The owner was startled when she unfolded the bag and found several live kittens.

Another extraordinary dog navigated miles of Iraqi minefields to follow a group of American soldiers who were relocating to a new post. The soldiers had befriended the lonely stray dog and fed him Pop Tarts. He wasn't about to be left behind.

These are just a couple of the many incredible dog stories I discovered that didn't make it into this book. During my research, I read hundreds of wonderful dog stories featuring loving, joyful, faithful, loyal, protective, resilient, and smart dogs.

My family has owned a few of these remarkable dogs.

My grandmother once adopted a stray dog that wandered into her yard in a small rural Arkansas town. The dog was big and shaggy, like an Old English sheepdog. He hung around and seemed to take a particular interest in her daughter, Mary Jane, who was two years old at the time. One day little Mary Jane was sitting on a blanket on the grass playing with toys while my grandmother worked nearby in the garden. The dog started growling and whining so my grandmother ran over to check on her toddler. The dog was there, next to the blanket, violently shaking a black snake that was in its mouth. It was a water moccasin, a very aggressive viper with a deadly bite. That stray dog saved the little girl who would one day become my mom.

When I was a kid we had an Australian shepherd-wolf dog mix named Boots that was black with golden feet. One night when I was about seven, Boots started barking frantically in the backyard. My dad peeked out the window and spotted a figure in black clothes crawling along the back fence. Boots barked some more, then silence. My dad heard a large grunt and a muffled exclamation. Boots had pounced on the potential intruder, who quickly decided to abandon our yard.

I'm pretty sure every dog lover has a favorite dog and a favorite story. But not all dogs are heroes. Not every dog story is warm and fuzzy. While dogs can be amazing, they can also drive us insane and shred our nerves with their Milk Bone-scented dog breath. For every dog that saves a baby or a kitten, there is a dog that barks insanely at squirrels or tries to eat baby birds that fall out of the nest. For every dog that survives abuse to become a calm and loving companion, there is a dog who joyfully jumps on everyone in sight, leaving muddy paw prints on white linen pants and red scratches on the bare legs of children. And for every dog that waits patiently by the door or gate, there is a dog with wanderlust who sprints out the door, takes a quick look back, and then takes off, running down the street for the start of a sweet doggie adventure.

My life as a dog owner has been more *Marley and Me* than *The Dog Whisperer*. Dogs rack up vet bills, chew things up, eat a lot, and poop. They bark, pull on the leash, and sometimes even bite. And then, just when you get them trained and you become really attached, your dog turns gray around the muzzle and ages right in front of your eyes. A dog's brief lifespan is one of life's great injustices.

So why do we do it? Plenty of people choose to own an iguana or a tank full of brightly colored fish. Why dogs? The answer is unconditional love. Dogs don't demand much. Pretty much all they want is to be near us.

More Than Just Dogs

Last year, the friendship of my dogs became even more important when I was diagnosed with breast cancer. Immediately I was swept into a roller-coaster ride of doctor visits and medical appointments. I had several diagnostic tests, two surgeries, chemotherapy, and radiation. Having cancer is like a demanding and time-consuming new career that a person isn't quite prepared for and certainly didn't want. The experience engulfed our family and stirred up a legion of fears and painful memories.

Several of my close relatives have died from various types of cancers, including my dad. He was an amazing father, and I adored him. A Texas cowboy, he survived a horrific childhood where both parents died, and he ended up an orphan at 15. He quit school to help support his two younger brothers, met and married my mom at 19, and with her support went to night school to get his high school diploma. He applied to Texas A&M, graduated with honors, and moved out to California to work for Safeway. He built a new life in the Golden State and provided my sister and me with an idyllic outdoorsy upbringing. He loved horses, and I grew up on a string of fat and friendly ponies. My favorite memories are of trail rides with him in the gorgeous green foothills surrounding our house. He was active, fit, and happy. He loved life, and he loved us.

But when he was 45 he contracted kidney cancer. And when he was 47, despite surgery, radiation, and chemo, the cancer advanced into his liver and he died quickly.

So when I had my first indication that there might be something dangerous lurking in my breast, the ghosts stirred. Fearful memories of illnesses and deaths dusted themselves off and came back to life. Long forgotten images and conversations and smells and sounds came to mind, unbidden and unwelcome.

At a women's retreat in the Santa Cruz mountains I had the time to think and grieve and cry and argue with God. This was so unfair. How could He do this to my family and me? Why did I have to go through this? I explained to God that I didn't have time for cancer. I'm writing books and speaking and doing ministry. I'm raising kids and being a wife and living my life. I'd been working out in the months previous, living and eating healthy. I was mentoring a budding speaker and teaching a women's Bible study. The retreat speaker, a gorgeous and wise woman, shared a Bible verse that rocked me. She talked about Philippians 4:6-7:

> Don't worry about anything, but pray about everything. With thankful hearts offer up your prayers and requests to God. Then, because you belong to Christ Jesus, God will bless you with peace that no one can completely understand. And this peace will control the way you think and feel.

Another translation reads: "Be anxious for nothing...And the peace of God, which surpasses all comprehension, will guard your hearts and your minds in Christ Jesus" (NASB).

I clung to that verse like a blind woman stumbling down a dark hallway. I memorized it, repeated it, and let it soak in. I did what it said. I prayed and thanked God for all the ways He has blessed me. I told Him my worries and my deepest, darkest thoughts. And slowly... slowly...it worked. It doesn't make much sense, but I began to experience peace.

I realized I am not my father.

My cancer is not my father's cancer.

Two very simple statements, but the journey I undertook to be able to say them, to think them, to believe them, was perilous. And I was helped along, in part, by my dogs. For most of my life dogs have been like furniture. Always there—happy, loveable, ready to play or take a walk. I took them for granted. But when I faced down cancer, our two dogs became more than just dogs. They became friends. And they did it gracefully and graciously, as dogs do. *It's no big deal,* I could almost hear Sprinkles and Eli thinking. *It's just what we do. We take care of blisters.*

Eli is our other dog, a big galumph of a chocolate Labrador retriever. He's the English type, broad and barrel-chested. He's as gentle as Ferdinand the Bull and just about as strong. If you experience the business end of his tail wagging, you will not soon forget it. He keeps a pile of big sticks by his bed, and every day before he goes out for a walk, he stops, considers his collection of sticks, and thoughtfully picks one to carry on the trails. He lugs the stick for miles, never dropping it. He is serious about his work and about as focused a fetcher as you will ever see. Throw that boy a ball and he will find it, no matter where it falls. He is rough and tough and rugged.

Three days after my lumpectomy, when my bandages were still new and white, I decided to go for a short walk on the trails. My husband and kids went with me. One of them had Eli on a leash, but he seemed to want to be close to me. He kept pulling at his leash to get near but I wasn't really paying attention.

We had walked a few steps when he quickly wheeled around, stood up on his hind legs with his paws on my shoulders, and looked me in the face. Now one thing you have to know about Eli is that he never jumps up. We've had our share of jumping dogs, and obviously God kept tabs and finally blessed us with a well-mannered dog. Even when he was a puppy, Eli seemed to understand that he wasn't supposed to jump up on us. But this time he jumped. And while he was standing on his hind legs, he dipped his head down and touched the exact spot on my breast where the surgeon had dug out the tumor. He gave me a gentle nudge with his nose, a quick lick, and then dropped to the ground.

It didn't hurt. The whole experience lasted just a few seconds. I was shocked at first and couldn't quite believe what he'd done. It wasn't like him. I thought all he really ever wanted from me was to feed him, give him treats, and throw things for him to fetch. But this was something more. It was like an anointing in a way, a quick doggie kiss to say, *I know you've been hurt, but you're going to be okay. And I care. I'll be here when you need me. Always.*

Dogs Being Dogs

Dogs love us. They just want to hang out with us. And dogs are willing to do just about anything to have a relationship with us. Every once in a while a dog pulls off a heroic feat, but more often they just want a soft place to sleep near us.

A friend told me a story about running in her first marathon with a few friends. She ran slowly, more of a waddle than a run. At one point during the race she found herself completely alone. As she ran, she felt lonely and began to wonder if she was even on the right road. Then a small white butterfly appeared, fluttering gently up and down at eye level next to her as she ran. Watching the butterfly put a smile on her face and gave her a boost. But then something strange happened; the butterfly stayed. For three or four miles, the butterfly flew by her side. It was just what she needed, and she went on to finish the marathon. The beautiful and fragile little insect had done something her friends could not.

Dogs, most of whom are not and never will be extraordinary, are with us in the race. My dogs will probably never lead me to safety from under the shadow of a collapsing skyscraper or take a poisonous snakebite for me, but they will sit by me in the backyard. They'll chase a ball, greet my friends with wagging tails, and wait patiently for a walk while I finish my lunch. They'll kiss my hurts and make me smile. They're just dogs being dogs. And that's enough.

Great Animal Organizations

If you're looking for a new pet or an organization to support, the animal organizations mentioned in these stories are worthy sources.

Alaska Dog and Puppy Rescue
PO Box 876888
Wasilla, AK 99687
907-745-7030
http://www.akdogandpuppyrescue
.com/

Coastal German Shepherd Rescue
PO Box 50726
Irvine, CA 92619-0726
714-528-4730
http://www.coastalgsr.org/

Guide Dogs for the Blind
350 Los Ranchitos Road
San Rafael, CA 94903
415-499-4000
http://www.guidedogs.com/

High Sierra Pet Rescue
PO Box 548
Portola, CA 96122
530-832-HSAR (4727)
http://www.highsierraanimalrescue.org/

Humane Society of America
2100 L St., NW
Washington, D.C. 20037
202-452-1100
http://www.humanesociety.org

Orthopets: Custom Orthotic Prosthetic
Mobility Solutions
886 East 78th Street
Denver, CO 80229
303-953-2545
http://www.orthopets.com/

Search Dog Foundation
501 East Ojai Avenue
Ojai, CA 93023
888-459-4376
http://www.searchdogfoundation.org/

SonRise Equestrian Foundation
PO Box 3097
Danville, CA 94526
925-838-RIDE (7433)
http://sonriseequestrianfoundation.org/

Tony La Russa's Animal Rescue Foundation
2890 Mitchell Drive, P.O. Box 30215
Walnut Creek, CA 94598
925-256-1273; 800-567-1273
http://www.arf.net/

Unchain Your Dog
http://www.unchainyourdog.org

Dog Books I Love

Day, Alexandra. *Good Dog, Carl.* New York: Aladdin Paperbacks, 1997.

Grogan, Josh. *Marley & Me.* New York: Harper, 2005.

Herriot, James. *James Herriot's Favorite Dog Stories.* New York: St Martin's Press, 2005.

Keller, Phillip. *Lessons from a Sheep Dog.* Waco, TX: Word, 1983.

Lee, Allyn, text, and illustrations by Connie Forslind's 2nd Grade Class, Rancho Romero School, 2010. *A New Job for Pearl.* Alamo, CA, www.anewjobforpearl.org.

McMorris, Mega, ed. *Woman's Best Friend: Women writers on the dogs in their lives.* Berkeley, CA: Seal Press, 2006.

Meeder, Kim, and Laurie Sacher. *Blind Hope: An Unwanted Dog and the Woman She Rescued.* Colorado Springs: Multnomah, 2010.

Millan, Cesar, and Melissa Jo Peltier. *Be the Pack Leader.* New York: Harmony 2007.

Mowat, Farley. *The Dog Who Wouldn't Be.* New York: Bantam, 1984.

Sparks, Bev. *The Life and Times of a Dog Lover.* Eugene, OR: Harvest House, 2009.

Steinbeck, John. *Travels with Charley in Search of America.* New York: Penguin, 2002.

Stringfellow, Jude. *With a Little Faith,* 2nd ed. Bloomington, IN: Xlibris, 2006.

Notes

Chapter 1: Buddy's Big Adventure

1. Richard Hunt, "Sea 'tail' has happy ending," *Fleetwood Today*, July 30, 2008, www.fleetwoodtoday.co.uk/fleetwood/sea-39tail39-has-happy-ending.4335093.jp, accessed Oct. 21, 2010.

Chapter 2: Champ and the .45

1. "Why Do Dogs Growl?" *Professor's House*, nd, http://www.professorshouse.com/pets/dogs/why-do-dogs-growl.aspx, accessed Oct. 21, 2010.

2. "Gangs," Los Angeles Police Department, http://www.lapdonline.org/search_results/content_basic_view/1396, accessed Oct. 21, 2010.

Chapter 3: Don't Mess with the Brute

1. Alex Leary, "Just Call Him National Hero Dog," *St. Petersburg Times,* May 6, 2004.

Chapter 4: Faith on Two Feet

1. "Faith is believing when common sense tells you not to. Don't you see? It's not just Kris that's on trial, it's everything he stands for. It's kindness and joy and love and all the other intangibles," spoken by Maureen O'Hara as Doris in *Miracle on 34th Street* (directed by George Seaton, 1947, based on a novel by Valentine Davies). This Oscar-winning film tells the story of a nice older man who claims to be Kris Kringle/Santa Claus.

Chapter 5: Freddie Takes Fight

1. Deborah Richie, "Raptor Festival Highlights Golden Eagle Flyway," *Bozeman Daily Chronicle* (Montana), Oct. 2, 1996.

Chapter 7: Hunter the Brave

1. "New Improved Explosive Detection Technology," *Armed Forces News,* Armed Forces International, June 2010, http://www.armedforces-int.com /news/new-improvised-explosive-detection-technology.html, accessed Oct. 21, 2010.

Chapter 8: Leo's Bathroom Buddies

1. Associated Press, "Hidden Victims of Mortgage Crisis: Pets," MSNBC.com, Jan. 29, 2008, http://www.msnbc.msn.com/id/22900994.

2. Ibid.

3. Sharon L. Peters, "Foreclosures Slam Doors on Pets, Too," *USA Today,* July 9, 2008, http://www.usatoday.com/news/nation/environment/2008 -03-24-foreclosures-pets_N.htm.

4. Lily Gordon, "Dog Is Columbus Woman's Hero," *Columbus Ledger-Enquirer* (Ohio), March 17, 2006, http://www.redorbit.com/news/science/432409 /dog_is_columbus_womans_hero_bull_mastiff_mix_pulled_attacker.

Chapter 10: Papa Loves You Kaiser

1. Chip Yost, "Homeless Vet, Best Friend Reunited," *KTLA News,* July 31, 2008, http://www.chicagotribune.com/news/local/blotter/ktla-vet-dog-re united,0,2897868.story.

2. Moira Anderson Allen, "Ten Tips on Coping with Pet Loss," *Pet Loss Support Page,* Pet Loss, nd, http://www.pet-loss.net, accessed October 20, 2010.

Chapter 11: Polishing the Black Pearl

1. Lisa Wade McCormick, "Rescued Dogs Become Rescuers," *Consumer Affairs,* Jan. 16, 2010, http://www.consumeraffairs.com/news04/2010/01/haiti_rescue _dogs.html, accessed Oct. 22, 2010.

2. Sharon Rice, "Heroes Heeded Call to Work in Haiti," *The Friday Flyer,* Feb. 12, 2010, http://calfire.blogspot.com/2010/02/ground-shook-my-daddy-went -my-dads-hero.html, accessed Oct. 22, 2010.

Chapter 13: Sophia in Wonderland

1. "Lucky the Dachshund Rescued from Badger Hole," *Dog Blog,* Nov. 2, 2009, http://dogblog.dogster.com, "Lucky the Dachshund," accessed Oct. 22, 2010.

Chapter 17: You Can't Catch Me

1. Stanley Coren, "What Do Dogs Know?" in *The Intelligence of Dogs,* nd, http://www.stanleycoren.com/e_intelligence.htm. Dr. Coren is a professor of psychology at the University of British Columbia. His bestselling book *The Intelligence of Dogs* contains a fascinating description of how dogs think, their mental abilities, and the various types of dog intelligence. One of its most controversial but intriguing findings is the systemic and regular differences among the dog breeds in their working and obedience intelligence. These findings, and the list ranking the relative intelligence of dog breeds, became front page news in newspapers around the world.

More Great Devotional Books
Featuring Animals
from Harvest House Publishers

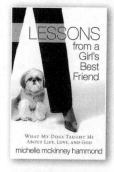

Other Great Harvest House Books

GOD, I'M READY TO WALK IN FAITH
Thelma Wells

Dynamic speaker and author Thelma "Mama T" Wells tackles the tough issues to help you strengthen your faith, develop a better grasp of the hope you have in Christ, and find joy and contentment in every day. She candidly shares her struggles and triumphs to reveal how to

- draw closer to God and learn more about who He is
- pray over the dreams He gives you and patiently wait for His guidance
- weed out lurking enemies of faith, including pride, greed, ego, and temptation

With her upbeat attitude and energetic faith, Mama T encourages you by providing questions to help you evaluate where you are and move confidently into a deeper relationship with God.

RUNNING WITH JOY
Ryan Hall

From the fastest American-born marathoner of all time, here is an intimate, day-by-day account of what it takes—physically, mentally, emotionally, and spiritually—to train for the peak of human performance. It also reveals the spiritual journey of an elite athlete who is a passionate follower of Jesus Christ. Discover how Ryan deals with injuries and illness, bad weather, disappointing workouts, and a slavish focus on results that can take the fun out of running. Whether you're a runner or a spectator, you'll be inspired by Ryan's quest for joy and his goal of glorifying Christ.

THIRSTING FOR GOD
Gary L. Thomas

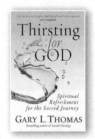

Are you tired of trying to live on the spiritual equivalent of fast food? Where can you turn for trustworthy guidance into a closer walk with God? This fascinating and easy-to-read journey into the insights of Christian leaders from centuries past will help you...

- set meaningful goals for your spiritual life
- overcome temptation and develop authentic holiness
- survive and even thrive in desert times

Discover what Christia   **31901050715533**   evant Christian walk
has nothing to do with   God.